MW01515776

To Tom,
With deep *[illegible]* *[illegible]* *[illegible]*
mentorship and friendship over the years.
Best regards,
Will

ORIGINS OF
PROFESSIONAL
PSYCHOLOGY

IN CANADA (1925–1965):

REFLECTIONS OF A PIONEER

BY EDWARD C. WEBSTER
WITH WILLIAM G. WEBSTER AND DAVID E. G. WEBSTER

 FriesenPress

One Printers Way
Altona, MB R0G 0B0
Canada

www.friesenpress.com

Copyright © 2023 by Edward C. Webster
First Edition — 2023

Editors: William G. Webster and David E.G. Webster

All rights reserved.

No part of this publication may be reproduced in any form, or by any means, electronic or mechanical, including photocopying, recording, or any information browsing, storage, or retrieval system, without permission in writing from FriesenPress.

Source of the partial newspaper clipping on the front cover:
Montreal Daily Star, June 16, 1936.

ISBN
978-1-03-917892-2 (Hardcover)
978-1-03-917891-5 (Paperback)
978-1-03-917893-9 (eBook)

1. PSYCHOLOGY, HISTORY

Distributed to the trade by The Ingram Book Company

Dedicated to the memory
of Inez Webster,
devoted wife, mother, and grandmother of the author and editors,
who was a source of support and encouragement for Edward Webster
during the years, and more, covered by these reflections.

TABLE OF CONTENTS

CHAPTER 6

Early Professional Psychologists and the CPA:

PREFACE

Edward C. Webster, 1909–1989

THESE REFLECTIONS FOCUS ON THE ORIGINS of professional psychology in Canada and on its early practitioners as seen through the eyes of one of the pioneers of the profession—the late Edward C. Webster.

An obituary of Edward Webster, written by Dr. Patricia M. Rowe of the University of Waterloo, one of his former doctoral students, has been included at the end of this Preface as a means of introducing the reader to the nature and the breadth of Edward Webster's interests in and his contributions to the profession.

Edward Webster began drafting these reflections in the early 1980s, but they were not completed before ill-health took its toll and he died in February 1989 at the age of 80. The draft chapters drew in part upon his recollections of a half-century of experiences during the early years of professional psychology in Canada. They also drew from the more recent days he had spent reviewing material in the Archives of the Canadian Psychological Association (CPA) in Ottawa (including reviewing relevant sections of the *Oral History of Psychology in Canada* by Dr. C. Roger Myers, 1975–1980) and analyzing membership directories of the CPA. During his work on the manuscript, Edward Webster shared sections of it with several of his contemporaries, who are discussed in the text and all of whom are now deceased. Their comments and observations very much influenced the shape of parts of the manuscript.

Much of the book is focussed on the individuals who were part of the origins, early struggles, and even stigma of the profession. It is our hope that this account, which is somewhat autobiographical, may bring to life these interesting times and the committed early Canadian psychologists who populated them. Their stories and contributions need to be preserved.

Following a discussion of what and who is a "professional psychologist," this account covers a period from the first appearance of professional psychology in Canada, well before World War II, until the mid-1960s at the time of the pivotal Couchiching Conference on Professional Psychology. The proceedings of that conference were summarized by Edward Webster in 1967 in the book *The Couchiching Report: Training in Professional Psychology in Canada*. A theme running through the last half of the present book relates to the interplay between the emergence of psychology as a profession and the development of the CPA from the war years through the mid-1960s.

Edward Webster was the father and grandfather of the two editors, William Webster (WGW) and David Webster (DEGW), respectively. The chapters he had drafted remained untouched for over 30 years after his death, when WGW, executor of his estate, found them among his effects. As a retired academic psychologist, WGW recognized their potential significance for professional psychologists and so, together with DEGW, proceeded to compile the material in the present book.

Except for the latter portion of Chapter 6 that we found in rough note form, and with the further exception of "Editors' notes" inserted mainly into Chapter 4, the chapters are presented more or less as they had been drafted. Most of the notes were prepared to provide information from now declassified military sources relevant to issues Edward Webster had raised concerning psychology in the war years.

We thank Dr. Patricia Rowe for allowing us to include her obituary of Edward Webster and for connecting us with Dr. Joseph (Jay) Howard, son of Dr. James Howard, who is discussed at some length in Chapter 4. Jay was most helpful to us tracking down information in the National Archives about his father. Also, we are pleased to acknowledge the assistance of Reiko (Webster) Fuentes to her grandfather, Edward Webster, in translating various French language documents he used during his drafting of Chapter 5. We also greatly appreciate that my (WGW) good friend and Dalhousie University colleague, Dr. Joseph Byrne, a professional psychologist himself, kindly read a very early version of the manuscript and provided encouraging and highly supportive comments about the value and significance of the project we had started.

This is Edward Webster's story. It is our hope that despite our editing and adding some additional commentary, the book has retained the authenticity of Edward Webster, his voice, his time, and his perspectives. His story was unfinished in its preparation. It is also unfinished in terms of a consideration of how the professional psychologists who practised during the first 40 years of the profession influenced and shaped the subsequent 60 years until today. That will be someone else's story for tomorrow.

William G. Webster, PhD
David E.G. Webster, MKin, MBA

OBITUARY OF
EDWARD C. WEBSTER, 1909–1989

(Reprinted from *Canadian Psychology/Psychologie canadienne*, Volume 31, No. 2, pages 180–181, Copyright © 1990 by the Canadian Psychological Association Inc.

Permission from the Canadian Psychological Association Inc. to reprint full article.)

EDWARD C. WEBSTER, RECIPIENT OF THE 1982 Distinguished Award for Contributions to Canadian Psychology as a Profession and Professor Emeritus of McGill University, died on February 15, 1989. His career was dedicated to the application of psychological principles to real life problems, not just in practice but in research, in administration, and in service to his profession and community.

Ed Webster was born in North Battleford, Saskatchewan, on January 13, 1909, but travelled east to study at McGill and stayed there for most of his professional career. He earned his BA in 1930, his MA in 1933, and the second PhD granted in Psychology by McGill in 1936. He joined the faculty of the Psychology Department in 1946 after a few years of industrial experience and wartime morale research in the Canadian Army and became chairman of the department in 1958, serving until 1964. He was named Professor Emeritus following his retirement in 1972. Throughout his lengthy academic career, Ed maintained an active consulting practice, opening an office in Montreal in 1934 before completing his doctorate and continuing his consulting work long into his retirement in Mississauga.

Like many of his generation, Ed Webster emerged from the war years committed to making a better world. He saw psychology as playing an important role in that world and was determined to promote and develop applied psychology in Canada. To this end he became the major proponent of applied psychology at McGill and established the Applied Psychology Centre from which grew both McGill's programme in clinical psychology and the McGill Guidance Service. His administrative talents were utilized, and applied psychology advanced when he served, at various times, as Director of the Applied Psychology Centre, the Guidance Service, the Industrial Relations Centre, and the Centre for Continuing Education at McGill.

Although committed to the development of applied psychology generally, Ed's major impact on theory and research was in industrial psychology, particularly in personnel selection. Like many other practitioners, he made extensive use of the interview as an information gathering technique upon which recommendations to hire were based. Yet he was aware of the mounting evidence of the lack of reliability and validity of the interview, and thus he sought to examine the discrepancy between research and practice in a major project funded by the Defence Research Board. That project involved five doctoral dissertations and several other studies that were published in 1964 in his book, *Decision Making in the Employment Interview*. The book has become a classic in industrial psychology and is credited with completely redirecting theory and research on the selection interview. Literally hundreds of research studies were inspired by what has become known as the McGill Studies on the interview. By bringing ideas from cognition and social psychology to bear on the processes of decision making in selection, Ed Webster was almost solely responsible for a shift from qualitative to quantitative analysis of the interview.

In what can only be a model for those who fear retirement, Ed published a new book on the interview in 1982, *The Employment Interview: A Social Judgment Process*. This book, which represents an updating and revision of the earlier one in light of the studies published in the intervening years, has already stimulated a number of studies and is regarded as a significant contribution to the selection literature.

Perhaps the best evidence of Ed's influence in his area is a recent book edited by Eder and Ferris, *The Employment Interview: Theory, Research, and Practice,* which has contributions from 30 authors. Not only do the editors provide a special acknowledgement of the inspiration provided by Webster's two books but also many of the chapters include a specific reference to his work. Finally, a special symposium dedicated to the impact of Ed Webster's work and to the future of research on the interview will be held in 1990 at the meeting of Division 14, the Society for Industrial and Organizational Psychology, of the American Psychological Association. Ed was himself a fellow of that division.

Another major contribution he made to Canadian professional psychology was undoubtedly the role he played in the Couchiching Conference on the training of applied psychologists, which culminated in the book he wrote in 1967, *The Couchiching Report: Training in Professional Psychology in Canada*. That report provided the basis for much of the development of graduate programmes in the applied areas in Canadian universities.

In his retirement he turned his attention to genealogy, particularly his own ancestry. Travels to England, Scotland, and Ireland, and research in the Ontario archives resulted in three mimeographed works, the last one completed just before his death. His work in this area will surely be greatly valued by his family and the generations to follow.

Those of us who were his students will always remember his challenges as to what our research really meant and how it could be put into practice, his encouragement when everything seemed to be going wrong, and our thesis discussions in his office filled with cigar smoke. And who will ever forget his prowess in arm wrestling?

In the 1950s Ed wasn't sure that women should be in graduate school, but he was honest and straight-forward in his opinion, and once he accepted a student he gave his unconditional support. He worked long hours and was in his office 6 days a week, and he expected the same from his students. The best time to see him was early in the morning or on Saturday. Then he was able to relax from his cares as chairman and the demands on his time from academic and consulting matters and give his undivided attention to the ideas and findings emerging from the student's work.

Ed was quick to adopt contemporary ideas, technology, and attitudes. He bought and taught himself to use a computer to aid him in his retirement work.

And when his devoted wife, Inez, died in 1982 and Ed was left alone, he accused his female friends and colleagues of being sexist if we asked too many questions about his cooking or cleaning skills. Indeed, he soon learned and reported with glee the virtues of cooking in quantity and dividing into portions that were frozen for later consumption.

He was a kind and generous man, contributing from his own funds to McGill's Psychology Department and later donating his personal library to the Industrial/Organization Ph.D. programme at the University of Waterloo. And he contributed his time and skill to his community as a member of the board of several Montreal social service agencies.

Ed Webster will be long remembered for his commitment to and promotion of applied psychology at McGill and in Canada, for his contributions to the literature in personnel selection, and for his support of the work of students and colleagues.

Patricia M. Rowe
University of Waterloo

ABOUT THE EDITORS

William G. Webster, BSc (McGill), MA (Cornell), PhD (Pennsylvania State), is a retired professor of psychology at Carleton University and Brock University, and a retired professor of communication sciences and disorders at the then University of Western Ontario and at Dalhousie University. He also served for 10 years as dean of the Faculty of Social Sciences at Brock University, and 11 years as dean of the Faculty of Health Professions at Dalhousie University. Apart from his more recent interest in, and contributions to, interprofessional health education, his primary research interests have focussed on the neuropsychology of stuttering and the management of speech by people who stutter.

David Webster holds a BA (psychology, business) from Mount Allison University, a Master of Kinesiology degree from Wilfrid Laurier University, and an MBA degree from St. Mary's University in Halifax. He currently works as an investment analyst at a major financial institution in Calgary

CHAPTER 1

DEFINITION AND OVERVIEW

THE VISION OF JAMES MCKEEN CATTELL

IN A 1937 ADDRESS, JAMES MCKEEN Cattell (1860–1944) quoted from a 1904 speech (Cattell, 1904) in which he had predicted the appearance of a profession based on the science of psychology. He had noted that a function of many professionals and businessmen is, to a considerable extent, that of an amateur psychologist. He foresaw the day when expert psychologists would be trained in professional schools comparable to those of medicine and would be paid for expert psychological services. That time had not arrived in 1904, and Cattell accepted the idea that, for the present, the psychological expert should be a member of a recognized profession who had specialized training in and a definite knowledge of psychology. He was, however, optimistic as to the future: "But in the end, there will not only be a science but also a profession of psychology" (Cattell, 1904, p. 186). He visualized the profession developing in a number of directions by means of a training model comparable to that which produced physicians.

Cattell's predictions have been fulfilled in the United States and Canada. Most graduate departments of psychology offer programmes designed to produce professionals as well as academic and basic scientists, even though few training models are similar to those in faculties of medicine. In the United States, a large proportion of professionals trained to work in health-related areas are being produced by free-standing schools of psychology. At the same time, it must be recognized that growth has been both slow and uneven, not only across the continent, but even within individual provinces and states.

WHAT AND WHO IS A PROFESSIONAL PSYCHOLOGIST?

The most obvious evidence of this diversity of training models is the fact there is no accepted definition of a "professional psychologist." The American Psychological Association has provided definitions for a number of professional specialties, but not for the profession as a whole. Individuals have made the attempt at definition, but I, personally, am unhappy with their efforts. Donald Peterson (1923–2007), who has been more closely associated with the development of health-care psychologists in American universities than anyone, described the profession in a very broad fashion: "A fully useful professional psychology is the discipline concerned with the assessment and functioning of human beings as individuals, in groups, or in social organizations" (Peterson, 1976, p. 793). This tells us little or nothing about the professional, but the need for a definition is critical if we are to have a useful consideration of the early professional psychologists.

Somewhat more satisfactory is the description by Fox, Barclay, and Rodgers (1982), who suggested that the professional "should be identified as dealing with areas of human need, which the underlying science of psychology attempts to understand and elucidate" (p. 307). They concluded that "a professional psychologist is one who has expertise in the development and application of quality services to the public in a controlled, organized, ethical manner based upon psychological knowledge, attitudes and skills in order to enhance the effectiveness of human functioning" (p. 307).

I do not quarrel with this definition, except it ignores an essential differentiation between many academics and genuine professionals: the latter earn their primary livelihood through their application of quality services based upon psychological knowledge, attitudes, and skills. The *Webster's Seventh New Collegiate Dictionary* (Merriam-Webster, Incorporated, 1971) gives its second definition of professional as "participating for gain or livelihood in an activity or field of endeavor often engaged in by amateurs; engaged in by persons receiving financial return." As far back as 1904, Cattell had specified financial return for expert psychological services as part of his definition.

This is an excellent definition, except it does not enable one to judge whether an individual is or is not a professional psychologist. The definition is not sufficiently explicit to provide guidelines as to what activities should be included in an account of the early days of professional psychology. Three additional conditions must be added to permit differentiation of a professional from an academic, a scientist, or an administrator:

- livelihood comes principally from the application of psychological knowledge, attitudes, and/or skills to enhance the effectiveness of human function;

- the individual must perceive himself/herself to be a psychologist; and

- the individual is licenced, certified, or registered in a province that requires non-academic psychologists to be so registered.

The significance of these practical deficiencies in the definition becomes apparent when we look at the development of professional psychology in the twentieth century. Our interest is in the Canadian scene, but this cannot be entirely separated from what took place south of the border. I will return to definition following a summary of stages in that development—a summary that anticipates the territory through which these present reflections will cross in the subsequent chapters.

STAGES OF DEVELOPMENT OF PROFESSIONAL PSYCHOLOGY

1. Almost from its beginnings, strong academic voices have assured the public that psychology can enable us to understand and solve a wide range of real-life problems. The notion of application not only went along with, but went ahead of advances in scientific knowledge. By the time the United States entered World War I, knowledge had laid a fairly sound foundation for the measurement of intellectual ability. This enabled American

psychologists to develop a system to screen and classify army recruits. They made other applications from perhaps less strong foundations.

2. The war's end brought a rush to extend the mental testing classification system to the civilian world. Industrial psychology experienced birth, a rapid growth that reflected high optimism, and a near death when it became evident expectations had been much higher than possible achievements. There was slower but better controlled application of mental testing to children. This contributed greatly to the development of both clinical and school psychology.

3. World War I had no direct impact on psychology in Canada except that it changed completely the orientation at the University of Toronto—and this certainly affected the discipline across most of the country. When a young instructor/graduate student, E. A. Bott (1887–1974) was rejected for military service in World War I, he turned the psychology department laboratory into a rehabilitation clinic and undertook the muscular re-education of wounded veterans. The clinic expanded and expanded. Bott was referred to as "Dr." in the university annual report, and the Royal Canadian Medical Corps appointed him "honorary captain." This wartime clinic established an applied direction to the department that continued until well after World War II. The history at McGill was quite different, but by the early 1930s, it had also developed an applied orientation, which lasted until about 1948. Other Canadian universities that had departments of philosophy and psychology remained "pure" between the two wars.

4. Individuals holding the position of "psychologist" in non-academic settings appear both in Toronto and Montreal by the late 1920s. Possibly two dozen such persons were employed across Canada by 1938; most were in Ontario and Montreal, but they were also found in British Columbia and Alberta and possibly in other provinces. These early professionals varied greatly both in academic background and in professional responsibilities. Two things they had in common—they were paid as professionals and were largely self-trained professionals.

5. World War II was a period when the whole Canadian community of psychologists turned to application. Some entered on military or government service; others remained in their academic setting but contributed

through applied research and/or very heavy teaching loads. These people, as a group, were not professionals. They were academics doing their duty in time of crisis. At the end of hostilities, most gladly returned to the university. Their war-time activities, however, changed the shape of Canadian psychology. Contributions were made to the Air Force, Navy, and various support groups, but the effort that involved the largest number of individuals was the selection and classification of army recruits. Many university graduates with various backgrounds were trained to be "army examiners." Quite a few joined the newly formed Canadian Psychological Association (CPA). Many on discharge sought admission to graduate school to become psychologists. Some wanted to be professionals, and it was they who provided the real impetus for a pressure group determined to develop a profession.

6. Chaos and controversy reigned for twenty years or more. Demands on university departments to provide training were great; resources were meager. Some departments developed professional programmes; some opted for pure science; some offered both professional and academic options; others had no firm objective but produced graduates at the master's level who, hopefully, had a better understanding of people. The 1945 to 1965 period was kind to psychology, particularly for the professional side.

7. Through these years, the CPA made serious efforts to help. Its founders may have been disconcerted when the first applications were received from non-academics, but by 1945, serious efforts were undertaken to control the use of the title "psychologist." It was quickly learned that control of professions lies solely within the provincial jurisdiction; the CPA then encouraged the establishment and growth of provincial psychological associations to oversee regulation. Many hours of volunteer time were given to the evaluation of records of members who sought acceptance by the American Board of Professional Psychologists.

8. In my opinion, the CPA's greatest contribution to all branches of Canadian psychology rests in efforts to direct training. The Canadian Social Science Research Council agreed to finance a cross-country examination of psychology in Canadian universities and colleges. In 1951, Professor Robert B.

MacLeod (1907–1972) of Cornell University undertook the study and reported in 1955 (MacLeod, 1955). He was negative not only in respect to what our universities were doing in undergraduate and graduate study but advised against professional training. He did recommend that a conference be held to develop a consensus among senior psychologists as to the desirable nature and direction of graduate training. This suggested a welcome opportunity to examine the professional side of psychology and its relation to graduate work directed towards academic goals.

9. The Canadian Psychological Association obtained a grant for such a conference, but to the dismay of those interested in the profession, the funding agency insisted that the direction be limited to research and academic training. The resulting Opinicon Conference (Bernhardt, 1961) held in 1960 undoubtedly produced a significant improvement in the quality of research in Canadian universities, but it created a significant split within the psychological community. To rectify matters, a second conference—this time specifically on professional training—was organized. Held in 1965 at Lake Couchiching, it provided a direction to training, particularly in the clinical area. For better or for worse, this direction has been maintained down to the time of writing this history (1980s). This present history and reflections, however, end with the Couchiching Conference (Webster, 1967) and its immediate aftermath.

THE PROFESSIONAL PSYCHOLOGIST: A WORKING DEFINITION

A working definition of "professional psychologist" in a history of and reflections on the professional scene must recognize changes in the profession that parallel the stages just summarized. The science has changed, as has the practice of the art, as well as the demands on the practitioner.

For purposes of this book, my definition of a "professional" accepts the suggestion of Fox et al. (1982), but with two important additions:

1. I agree, subject to factors related to place and time, the professional is one with expertise in the development and application of quality

service to the public, provided in a controlled and ethical manner, based upon psychological knowledge, attitudes, and skills prevalent and available at the time, in order to enhance the effectiveness of human functioning.

2. The professional is one who performs these operations in a non-academic psychology setting and looks to such work as the primary source of earned income. Such a person must act in ways that ensure public and personal identification as a psychologist. Normally this will include voluntary membership in a psychological association.

This working definition enables us to recognize as professionals persons who, particularly in the early days, possessed at best a bachelor's degree and restricted their activities to a narrow field such as mental testing. It effectively excludes both those who regard themselves as professors or research scientists. This leaves one grey area: administrators. My feeling is that such individuals should be accepted as professionals if they required training in psychology to obtain their position and have maintained an active connection with the community of psychologists.

CHAPTER 2

PROFESSIONAL PSYCHOLOGY BETWEEN THE TWO WORLD WARS

TWO CANADIAN UNIVERSITIES HAD DEPARTMENTS OF psychology by 1939: McGill (1924) and Toronto (1926). Both universities had provided instruction in psychology for years through their respective departments of philosophy. Other departments of psychology were established as separate entitles after 1945, with the exception of Université de Montréal, where the Institut de Psychologie opened in 1942 to provide instruction in "psychologie experiment-ale." It produced both academics and professionals from its early days.

No Canadian university attempted to produce professionals prior to World War II, although graduates from both Toronto and McGill became professionals with departmental support. Individual graduates of the University of British Columbia and Alberta showed up as professionals by the mid-1930s. Also, by that time, there were one or two professionals with degrees from the United States.

This history and reflections should be read in conjunction with the *History of Academic Psychology in Canada*, edited by M. Wright and C. R. Myers (1982). Generally accurate, it does contain some errors, particularly in respect to the early years. Most chapter authors had to rely on written documentation, which did not necessarily reflect reality.

EARLY PROFESSIONAL ACTIVITY ACROSS CANADA

This chapter focusses on the emerging profession in Quebec and Ontario. As will be discussed in Chapters 4 and 6, the seeds were sown shortly before 1939 and the outbreak of the war that would lead to the founding of the Canadian Psychological Association (CPA); this cannot be ignored because of its impact on the post-war profession.

First, however, we should dispose of evidence of early professional activity in other parts of the country: Alberta and British Columbia to be specific. Information has been obtained from CPA Archives and a few telephone calls. I hope I am not overlooking any pioneer professional.

Alberta established a number of child guidance clinics and, in 1931, employed Mr. Edward J. Kibblewhite (BA 1929, MA 1931, MEd 1936), a graduate of the University of Alberta. He had spent about a year in "mental hygiene work" at the mental hospital located in Ponoka, Alberta. Mr. Kibblewhite attended clinics in half a dozen centres in Southern Alberta. He initially had no title but later was asked which he preferred: social worker or psychologist. When interviewed by C. R. Myers in 1970 as part of the *Oral History of Psychology in Canada* project, he stated he chose "psychologist." This is interesting in view of the fact that he appears in the 1945 CPA Directory as "chief social worker, psychologist." Ten years later, he reported himself as "chief psychologist," but in 1966, he gave his title as "welfare officer." One does not know why, if clinics were opened about 1931 in Southern Alberta, they were not held in the northern or central region without a psychologist. He assured Myers he was the only psychologist in the Alberta public health service in pre-war years; there is no suggestion of psychologists in other professional settings.

British Columbia opened a child guidance clinic in 1935, which required a staff psychologist. The first appointee was Miss Barbara Robertson, BA (UBC), MA (McGill). Later she was well known as Mrs. N. Whitman Morton to all psychologists closely associated with personnel selection in the Canadian Army or with the Defence Research Board in its early years. Miss Robertson had a major accident in 1937 and retired from the work force. She was replaced as psychologist by Mr. Charles Watson, MA candidate at UBC, who obtained his degree in 1938 with a thesis on stuttering. Mr. Watson remained with the Child

Guidance Clinic until he entered the Army in 1942. In addition to guidance clinic activities, he operated a speech clinic, worked with the Young Offenders Unit, and did a limited amount of private practice on psychiatric referrals. There were, so far as is known, no other professionals in British Columbia.

THE QUEBEC SCENE

All professional psychology in Quebec was located in Montreal. Only McGill University offered a sufficient number of courses to permit "continuation," let alone honours or graduate work. With one real and one "faked" (falsified credentials) exception, all professionals until the war were McGill graduates or McGill supported.

This between-war period is reported in two sections: pre-1935 and post-1935. The reason for this division is personal. I opened an office as a consulting psychologist in 1935 and am much more confident of the accuracy and completeness of information for the latter period. For the earlier period, I rely on memories of things told to me and on correspondence during 1983–1985 with four "old-timers":

- Dr. Kay Banham (1897–), who, at age 89, was still giving evening lectures at Duke University and completing a translation of a French book on parapsychology to be published in 1985 [*Editors' note: Dr. Banham died in 1995*];

- Dr. Gerald P. Cosgrave, PhD from Toronto (1928), the first PhD professional in Canada and the only professional psychologist to receive two honorary degrees;

- Mrs. Gwendolyn P. Groves (nee Peden), BA from McGill (1930), MA (1935); and

- Mrs. Mary Korenberg (nee Cardon), BA from McGill (1927), MA (1929).

We are all reporting recollections and events that took place more than 50 years ago, and many of those events had no particular importance to us. There must be some errors or some omissions—particularly in the pre-1935 segment.

Even so, this is a most important period for anyone really interested in the beginnings of our profession—a very different profession from what quickly developed in the post-war period.

PRE-1935

Professionals and presumed professionals worked for one of four organizations that thought they were employing trained psychologists, although two were unwilling to use that title. These, in order by which they employed psychologists, were Sun Life Assurance Company of Canada; the Montreal Mental Hygiene Institute; J. Walter Thompson; and the Catholic School Commission of Montreal. There was one additional professional—Mr. F. R. Clarke—sponsored by Dr. W. D. Tait, chairman of the McGill Department of Psychology. He is described first although I am not sure when he became a professional— probably about 1927 or 1928.

MR. F. R. CLARKE

Mr. Clarke, a trained and experienced English newspaper reporter and columnist, came to Canada after World War I, worked for some years on Montreal newspapers, organized and managed a community supported employment agency for working-class men, and later was assistant to the personnel manager of Northern Electric Company. Schooling was limited, but he was a highly intelligent, self-educated, well-read individual, who expressed himself readily in speech and writing. He took the several non-credit evening courses offered by Dr. Tait during the 1920s and become interested in mental tests and vocational guidance.

By 1931, when I first heard of Mr. Clarke, Dr. Tait considered him to be a professional psychologist in the area of vocational guidance. It was in 1931 that the department moved towards applied research that involved mental testing of adults and school pupils. We graduate students were referred to Mr. Clarke for advice, but we found he was extremely naive in his thinking about tests. For example, we needed an "O'Connor Wiggly Block" (an oblong piece of wood cut into nine segments in a "wiggly" manner; the score was the time required to reassemble the block). McGill did not own this test, so we borrowed and used that belonging to Mr. Clarke. It was apparent we could test two people simultaneously if we had a second block. We borrowed one from Sir George Williams College and found it was quite different both in size and in "wiggles" from that of Mr. Clarke. He, it turned out, had had a picture of the block that he turned over to a woodworking friend who cut three: one that we had borrowed; one Mr. Clarke could carry in his vest pocket when he went to a home to give vocational guidance; and one (about three feet long) kept at the employment agency for use with working men. He applied the test publisher's norms to scores obtained from three models but was embarrassed to find that we disapproved of what he had done.

By courtesy of Dr. Tait, he was certainly an early professional psychologist. During the war years, he lectured on industrial psychology at the Institut de Psychologie, Université de Montréal, and he was an "associate member" of the CPA in 1945. He was probably the only person in Canada to buy a share of stock in the Psychological Corporation, New York, when this was offered sometime in the 1930s. He told me, in the late 1940s, when he gave me his share, that he did it "to encourage psychology."

I have described this rather unusual individual to set the stage for a description of the profession as it developed in the post-War I period. Mr. Clarke was accepted as a professional who restricted his activities to his thought-to-be area of competence.

DR. GERALD P. COSGRAVE

Like senior executives of many large American organizations, the president of Sun Life Assurance Company of Canada, one of McGill University's most powerful governors, had read about the contribution intelligence testing could make to a company. He wanted a psychologist on staff. There is confusion as to when this decision was reached, but in 1928, Sun Life approached Professor E. A. Bott, chairman of the department at the University of Toronto. Five names were suggested and Gerald P. Cosgrave, a new PhD, was offered employment. Professor Bott accompanied him to Montreal to study the offer; Cosgrave accepted. As a staff psychologist, he developed a number of ability and achievement tests for the company and did personnel research as well as research for other departments. Starting with a staff of five, his unit increased to seven or eight, including a woman with a MA degree from McGill. (A contemporary mentioned this lady by name and said she had gone to Sun Life "but with no fancy title.")

Cosgrave himself had "no fancy title"; he was personnel supervisor. He was very well paid for one with this title: $4300 per year at a time when beginning high school teachers were receiving $1500 and the McGill psychology chairman, a full professor, received $5000. Both figures were reduced when the depression settled in. However, Cosgrave's training as a psychologist was kept under cover. He understood that those who employed him had passed the word along privately, but there was to be no public recognition.

Cosgrave was not the first psychologist at Sun Life. A young MA candidate at Toronto, Karl Bernhardt (1901–1967) spent three months during the summer of 1928 studying absenteeism. More peculiar was that the Sun Life had employed a woman graduate in psychology from McGill. She had left; Cosgrave never met her. We do not know how long she was employed or her responsibilities. It must have been at least one year, perhaps two or three. She met and married a fellow worker, which necessitated her resignation. We know her name was Mrs. Crowe and that she went to the Mental Hygiene Institute, where she remained until 1930 when she left to raise a family.

It is clear that Sun Life had a trained psychologist on staff by 1927 and perhaps as early as 1925. The Depression seriously affected the company and Cosgrave left in 1932. He returned to the University of Toronto as an assistant professor but returned to professional life during the war years and, as will discussed in Chapter 3, made major contributions in the counselling area.

MRS. CROWE AND MISS GWENDOLYN PEDEN

The Montreal Mental Hygiene Institute was founded in 1919 to provide a psychiatric service for Montreal charities and schools. The original director, Dr. Murphy, retired about 1924 or 1925 to be replaced by Dr. T. W. Mitchell, who appointed a young MD from Toronto as "assistant psychiatrist and psychologist." The appointee, Dr. Baruch Silverman, had undoubtedly received courses in psychology from Professor J. W. Bridges.

We know Mrs. Crowe came to the institute as a psychologist by the summer of 1928. Her training and/or experience at Sun Life must have prepared her for the duties expected. She was called a psychologist and, as mentioned above, left in 1930 to raise a family. She was succeeded by Miss Gwendolyn Peden, a McGill BA (1930) who had been recommended by Dr. W. D. Tait. This recommendation is surprising, as he had a competent post-MA student who wanted to get into clinical psychology, yet he recommended the BA. One can only speculate as to the reason. A digression to describe the McGill programme in psychology may throw some light on the situation.

On the basis of course work, the two women almost certainly had equivalent training. The undergraduate programme included courses in statistics, abnormal psychology (until 1931), motivation, and mental testing (including a minimum training in the administration and scoring of the Stanford-Binet Test of intelligence). No other course, until the mid-1930s, could have any relevance to professional work. At the graduate level, there were only two regular courses: advanced statistics and a two-year seminar on William James. The thesis, of course, might be relevant depending on the topic. Ferguson (1982) gives an excellent description of the department before World War II; except he grossly exaggerates the importance of applied psychology.

Psychology from 1925 to 1933 was a two-man department. Dr. W. D. Tait, professor and chairman, liked to talk about how his science would solve practical problems and help people. Actually, he took no interest in anything applied. When, for example, in 1925 the Laura Spellman-Rockefeller Foundation established a nursery school and Child Study Laboratory at McGill, Dr. Tait would have nothing to do with it and would not permit graduate students to use it for research purposes. We have seen how Sun Life Assurance went to Toronto rather than McGill when looking for a psychologist. Dr. Tait directed my applied research but had no interest in anything but the style of my writing. He could not understand why I could not, or would not, develop as a thesis style the language of Edward Gibbon in *The Decline and Fall of the Roman Empire*.

The other staff member, Dr. Chester E. Kellogg, never showed any interest in anything applied, although his graduate student and, after 1933, fellow professor, N. Whitman Morton (1910–1976), more or less forced him to help develop a civilian version of the US Army Beta intelligence test on which Kellogg had worked during World War I. The department became involved with applied research in 1931, when Carnegie money established a social sciences research council that earmarked several thousand dollars a year to psychology for work in the area of employment. This money continued to be available at least until 1939.

To return to the Mental Hygiene Institute, its psychologist spent most of his or her time administering mental tests to pre-school and elementary-school children referred by agencies and schools. The standby test was the Stanford-Binet, but this was supplemented with various verbal and non-verbal measures, and with standardized achievement tests where appropriate. The psychologist also noted any interesting behaviour and would pass on all information to a psychiatrist for interpretation and use. This was still basically what the psychologist did at the Mental Hygiene Institute in 1948 or 1949. Miss Peden received her MA in 1935 and, the following year, moved to the United States, where she hoped to find more challenging work.

Another commercial organization, the J. Walter Thompson Advertising Agency, deliberately employed an individual in about 1931 partly because of her training in psychology. However, the person hired, Ms. Mary Cardon, identified with agency personnel, not with psychology, and therefore, as explained in Chapter 1, I cannot accept her as a professional psychologist. But her experience is an interesting example of life in the late 1920s and early 1930s.

MS. MARY CARDON

Miss Mary Cardon received her BA in psychology and her teacher's diploma from McGill in 1927. She taught school and registered for her MA; the thesis was in the area of education. She received the MA in 1929 and continued as a post-MA student for a year. Her hope was clinical psychology in which Professor J. W. Bridges had interested her. She saw no possibility of such work, and as she was getting married, she could no longer teach. She did what many ambitious women did: took a secretarial course and sought such work.

She happened to apply to J. Walter Thompson when it was looking for a secretary to the director of Research. The agency had recently brought the behaviourist, Dr. John B. Watson, onto the New York head office staff as a vice-president. The Canadian office felt it would not hurt to have a psychologist as secretary to the Montreal director of Research. A year or so later, this man was transferred to New York, and Miss Cardon was appointed acting director of Research. In due course, the "acting" was dropped from her title, and then the position of media director was added. She continued with J. Walter Thompson until retirement. She should have been a professional psychologist, but she never identified with any group of psychologists, although, sometime after World War II, she did discuss with me the question of becoming an academic psychologist. It was, in my opinion, much too late.

UNNAMED

One other organization sought to employ a psychologist in the pre-1935 period: the Catholic School Commission of Montreal. By the early 1930s, it had quite a number of classes for pupils with learning difficulties. They were under the direction of L'Abbe Lussier, later rector of Université de Montréal. He went to the United States to find a French-speaking PhD graduate in clinical-educational psychology. He found what appeared to be such a person, brought him to Montreal, and was satisfied with the quality of his work.

When the Institut de Psychologie was founded in 1936, L'Abbe Lussier suggested we bring this man in as an associate. Then, by accident, L'Abbe Lussier was talking to an academic and congratulated him on having produced such a PhD. It turned out the man employed had no degrees but had been an efficient technician in the clinic laboratory. That ended his position and acceptance as a psychologist, although, under a number of titles, he developed a clinical-counselling-industrial practice that continued for thirty years or more. This was a tragedy. The man's technical qualifications were certainly better than those of Mr. F. R. Clarke with whom we commenced this section. That said, I thought it best not identify him by name.

Professional psychology in Quebec and Montreal between 1935 and 1942 revolved around two individuals: Dr. J. S. A. Bois and myself. Our backgrounds need to be known.

DR. J. S. A. BOIS

Bois, a French-Canadian, learned English while a graduate student at McGill. Prior to this, he had been a Roman Catholic priest for some 15 to 20 years. Near the end of this period, he had been sent to Europe, received training in clinical therapy both within and outside the Church. On return to Quebec, he was a therapist approved to work with priests and nuns with emotional problems.

Difficulties arose, and he was relieved of his clerical duties and tried in a court of the Inquisition held in Quebec City. It required some five years to obtain a final disposition of the case from Rome. Bois earned a living tutoring students in Greek, Latin, and mathematics, and used the time to work towards his PhD in psychology at McGill. He obtained his MA in 1934 and PhD in 1936. Early in 1936, word was received from Rome that he was returned to civil status in good standing with the Church. Once this word was received, he and I started preparation for establishing psychology as a major profession. It should be noted here, as it proved very important, that while at McGill, Bois had been very active in a national political movement that had the objective of establishing Quebec as a republic.

DR. EDWARD WEBSTER

My background was the YMCA. I came to McGill after a year as the Boys Work secretary at the Y in Saskatoon, Saskatchewan, to complete my BA and to qualify as a secretary. During my two years of undergraduate study at McGill, I spent between 24 and 30 hours a week as the assistant Boys Work secretary of what is now the downtown YMCA. I became disillusioned with Y work when I discovered that the principal responsibility of a general secretary was to organize an annual financial drive.

Just at this time, the spring of 1931, a graduate student, N. Whitman Morton, told me the Department of Psychology received money from the Social Science Research Committee for research on unemployment and related subjects. He was going to study unemployment and suggested I apply. I did. For five years, I worked on problems related to vocational guidance and was a very (very) junior staff member. The Social Science Research Committee made money available for me to spend two months in 1933 studying vocational guidance at the National Institute of Industrial Psychology in London, England. While there, the director, Dr. C. S. Myers, former chairman of Psychology at Cambridge, assured me he would not employ a psychology graduate to be an industrial psychologist. In his view, they were too philosophical. He looked for persons with a good liberal arts undergraduate degree; the institute could assign reading and training to produce an industrial psychologist.

The summer of 1934 was spent operating a vocational guidance clinic for boys graduating from high school. It was very well received, and the next spring, I decided to open an office as a consultant psychologist in the area of vocational guidance. The following newspaper clipping, which is from the *Montreal Herald* on June 30, 1935, describes my objective under the headline "Psychologist Advises on Future Vocations."

Psychologist Advises On Future Vocations

The first office of a consultant psychologist to be established in Canada, specializing in vocational guidance, has been opened in Montreal at 4652 Sherbrooke street west by E. C. Webster, M.A., graduate of McGill University and student of the National Institute of Industrial Psychology of England.

The project, while of necessity of a commercial nature, has received the approval of McGill University authorities and its services have been recommended to parents having children about to enter university by Dr. W. D. Tait, chairman of the Department of Psychology at McGill.

REPORT TO PARENTS.

A searching examination of the "case" is made and an exhaustive reports of the capabilities and tendencies returned to the parents, with complete advice as to the bent of the youth in question and his possibilities of success in the profession recommended.

Last year out of 25 students who attended university, nine Mr. Webster had advised against entering that seat of learning. Of these nine, four failed, four were conditioned and one passed, and of the remaining 16 whom he had urged to continue their studies, thirteen passed, two were conditioned and one failed.

ELIMINATE MISFITS.

It is the psychologist's contention that the many occupational misfits, men dissatisfied with their work or a failure in their chosen lines can, in the main, be obviated by proper psychological examination which will result in directing their efforts into those channels for which they are best suited.

To date, as the work is of a pioneer nature, Mr. Webster has confined himself to the examination of boys — high school graduates who are not definitely sure which field of professional activity they wish to enter.

Fortunately, my office had been a physician's office in an apartment. He had died and his widow, a former psychology student, rented it furnished. While parents of high school graduates had been keen on referring their sons to a free clinic in 1934, they were not keen on a $15 fee in 1935. Income did not meet rent, and in the fall, my landlady permitted me to move into the office and use her kitchen for breakfast. I had afternoon and evening office hours certain days of the week until I received my PhD.

The spring of 1936 looked promising to establish a major facility in professional psychology. Bois and I decided to base our organization so far as possible on the National Institute of Industrial Psychology (NIIP). We selected the name "The Psychological Institute, L'Institut Psychologie" and obtained a Quebec charter as a non-profit organization. Offices were established in a top-quality office building. The following two newspaper clippings are from the *Montreal Daily Star* (June 16, 1936 and October 7, 1936) and describe the objectives, staff, and organization.

INSTITUTE OPENED BY PSYCHOLOGISTS

McGill University Experts To Campaign For Public Education

Continuing and extending pioneer work carried out in Montreal by Dr. W. D. Tait, chairman of the department of psychology at McGill University, two brilliant graduates of the department and members of the staff have inaugurated the Psychological Institute and will conduct a campaign of public education in the application of psychology to the solution of widespread industrial and family problems.

The campaign, to be carried out by Dr. E. C. Webster and Dr. J. S A. Bois, will follow along the lines of the successful work in England of the National Institute of Industrial Psychology, of London, which has philanthropic support of some of the leading educationists and industrialists of Great Britain and serves as a model for the local institute.

TO DIRECT INDUSTRY

The work in the realm of industry will largely be directed to the improvement of production and direction of industry through the better placement of both workers and executives. Scientific psychological tests devised and used in leading countries of the world will be employed in this work.

The work among families will largely be directed along the lines of assisting educationists in the installation of vocational tests in schools and co-operating individually with parents in the selection of suitable careers for their children.

Dr. Webster has studied for several months in London in this special field as well as having carried out extensive research here. Dr. Bois, a graduate of Laval University as well as of McGill, has studied clinical psychology in Paris, Rome and Boston. His chief work will be to introduce modified European psychological methods in clinical and consultative work into the French section of the province's population. The institute is the first of its kind in Canada.

INSTITUTE DIRECTORS AND ADVISORS NAMED

Psychology Officials Are Appointed

Names of the board of directors and the technical advisory board of the Psychological Institute, Montreal, who have just been appointed, were announced today at the institute as follows: Board of directors: Dr. S. A. Bois, M.A., Ph.D. president of the institute and consulting psychologist to the institute; Dr. E. C. Webster, M.A. Ph.D. secretary and treasurer of the institute and consulting psychologist to the institute; Dr. J. E. Reed, Dr. J. E. Noel.

Technical advisory board: Dr. W. D. Tait, chairman of the department of psychology, McGill University; Dr. C. E. Kellogg, associate professor of psychology, McGill University; Dr. A. A. Roback, Massachusetts University Extension, Boston; Dr. H. Bastien, faculty of philosophy, University of Montreal.

Associate psychologists to the institute: Dr. N. W. Morton. lecturer, department of psychology, McGill University; L. Chatel, psychologist to the Catholic School Commission, Montreal.

Newspaper clippings from the Montreal Daily Star on June 16, 1936, and October 7, 1936, announcing (left) the opening of the Psychological Institute and (right) the appointment of advisors and members of the board of directors.

THE PSYCHOLOGICAL INSTITUTE

The Psychological Institute had a place in the establishment of Montreal. Not only were all members of staff from the McGill Department of Psychology involved, but Dr. J. E. Reed was the director of the Verdun Protestant Hospital (a mental hospital) and Dr. J. E. Noel was a physician and managed a general hospital in Sherbrooke, Quebec.

Edward Webster testing a client at the Psychological Institute in 1936. (The photo was provided to me courtesy of the photo editor of the Montreal Daily Star, April 14, 1936.)

Our first objective was to ensure peace with the psychiatrists in the community. We had a four-hour meeting at which it was agreed psychologists could do as they wished with "cases," provided they did not pass on the mental state of the individual; only a psychiatrist could make a diagnosis of mental state. We agreed not to accept referrals from physicians other than psychiatrists, as such physicians would almost certainly want an assurance as to the mental state of the person referred. (It must be recognized that there were, in 1936, no more than one or perhaps two psychiatrists who had been training in this specialty; the others, about 15 or 20, were neurologists or family doctors who had self-trained.)

We promoted the application of psychology through newspaper columns and radio programmes. For more than two years, CBC and Mutual Radio stations carried my "Life's Like That" programme every Thursday afternoon. (The programme had an "interview" format; the interview had to be prepared in advance and read from script. I got paid $15 a week and my stooge interviewee received $5.) We sponsored two or three public lectures but lost too much money to justify this type of promotion.

We had to live, and this required a certain amount of money. Bois continued tutoring for a year or so. I had a windfall: Sir George Williams College required someone to teach their psychology courses, and from 1936 until 1940. I taught the only two offered, day and evening, 10 hours a week at $2 per hour. We both wrote books: Bois produced several popular texts in French and developed a correspondence course. Supported by the Social Science Research Committee of McGill, I published a rewrite of my PhD thesis (Webster, 1939) and I also wrote a book on self-guidance (Webster, 1941). This could not be reviewed on radio or in Canadian newspapers, as it was considered against our war effort—young men served their country; they did not think of what they should do in peacetime.

We worked long hours and struggled to broaden our areas of expertise. Bois became knowledgeable in the area of testing, and we both developed some skill in the use of both the Rorschach and TAT. I became quite comfortable teaching progressive relaxation as described by Jacobson of Chicago and habit modification in accordance with Knight Dunlap.

After a year, it did look as if we might have to give up by the end of 1937, but then Bois's earlier political connections paid off. The Federal-Provincial Youth Training Plan was expanded, and the Psychological Institute was given a contract to advise the government on training needs; to evaluate young people for training; and to supervise placement officers. Young people were evaluated through a 90-minute test battery to measure intelligence, clerical and mechanical ability, finger dexterity, and personality. It was administered to thousands over a two-year period.

Profits were used to broaden our activities. We failed in our attempt to have the Canadian Manufacturers Association sponsor a nationwide job description and evaluation plan that would enable companies to compare rates of pay for similar jobs. Almost from the beginning, we had built close relations with the Psychological Corporation in New York, and we were impressed with what they were doing in market research—an area where our statistics could be put to good use. With a promise of assistance and advice from the Corporation, we built a 150 to 200 interviewer network of schoolteachers employed by Opinion Surveys Limited. We undertook quarterly polls that included both opinion and consumer product questions. We also completed both regional and national surveys on behalf of individual organizations. This paid its way, and we brought in two psychologists: Mr. Hampton C. Shaw, MA, and Mr. Aurele Gagnon, MA.

Everything was going well through 1941. Professional psychology was established. A Columbia-trained child therapist, Dr. Frances Alexander, joined the Psychological Institute on a part-time basis. We had broadened the range of work by developing testing programmes for a few war industries, and companies were sending applicants to us for evaluation.

Bois and I regarded ourselves as generalists. Speaking on clinical psychology in 1945 at the Canadian Psychological Association meeting in Montreal, Bois drew upon his experiences during the first five years of the institute (1936–41) and provided a clear description of just how we regarded our role as professionals. He entitled his talk "The Field of the Psychological Therapist":

> The consulting psychologist is an advisor in matters of human behaviour. Behaviour disorders may appear over a wide area of human experience. They may be those of the infant whose eating or sleeping habits must be guided and supervised, or of the adolescent whose vocational choice must be kept in line with his degree of learning ability, his special aptitudes, and his total environment. They may be as well those of the individual, young or old, whose emotional habits are inadequate to meet a continuous or a catastrophic tension. In the latter cases the inadequacy of his emotional training may bring about one of two types of symptoms, or a combination of both: a) physiological disturbances such as

poor indigestion, circulatory dysfunctions, ulcers of the stomach, skin troubles etc., b) symptoms that are called "psychoneurotic": headaches, insomnia, amnesia, anxiety, ideas of reference, and so forth. When dealing with symptoms of the first type, we are apt to speak of psychosomatic medicine, and when dealing with those of the second type, we may speak of psychiatry. For the viewpoint of the consulting psychologist, this dichotomy is not necessary. He may look upon them all as problems of human behaviour that he attempts to solve in terms of aptitudes, personality traits, acquired habits, environment, emotional maturation, and other strictly psychological categories. His role as a therapist remains closely similar to his function as a vocational or educational counselor, an industrial psychologist, an analyst of trends of opinions, and to all other generally accepted functions of his profession (Bois, 1945a, p.70).

In a publication at about the same time, Bois (1945b) elaborated on the nature and approach of the Psychological Institute as an independent professional organization and provided more specific examples of the therapeutic approach.

As will be discussed in later chapters of these reflections, late in 1941, Bois was approached to enter the Canadian Army as one of the first group of army examiners. There was no other French-Canadian psychologist in Canada with an appropriate background. It was impossible to reject the request. I found myself putting in weeks of 100 hours, and when in June of 1942 I was requested to enter the Army to conduct morale research, I accepted. We believed we had arrangements that would ensure the continuation, on a reduced scale, of both the Psychological Institute and Opinion Surveys Limited. Unfortunately, conditions changed through nobody's fault, and we relinquished both charters within a year.

A number of developments during the war years deserve brief mention in this context:

- Dr. Frances Alexander took a wartime academic position at McGill and opened an office as a child therapist. She carried on in both roles until she left Montreal and returned to New York in 1947.

- About 1943, the Jewish Vocational Service was established in Montreal with Dr. Jacob Tuckman as director. By 1945, he had at least one additional psychologist on staff. The service made a much-needed contribution to the English-speaking community—Jew and Gentile alike.

- Also, by the end of the war, a management consulting firm of engineers, Stevenson and Kellogg, had psychologists on staff to recommend individuals who should be hired or promoted.

I have not been able to uncover useful information about the early days of these three ventures. But Dr. Alexander and Dr. Tuckman were instrumental in making contact with the new Institut de Psychologie at the Université de Montréal and founding the Psychological Association of the Province of Quebec. By late 1945, that association was drawing 100 or more people to its meetings.

CHAPTER 3

EARLY PIONEERS OF INDUSTRIAL/ ORGANIZATIONAL PSYCHOLOGY IN CANADA:

ISSUES OF IDENTITY, ROLE, AND TRAINING

"PERSONNEL PSYCHOLOGY"—THE FIRST NAME FOR INDUSTRIAL and organizational psychology—came to Canada in 1928 when, as discussed in Chapter 2, Dr. Gerald P. Cosgrave accepted the position of personnel supervisor in the employment department of Sun Life Assurance Company's head office in Montreal. The company president had read an article on the practical value of the Stanford-Binet test and sought a psychologist through Professor E. A. Bott, chair of the Department of Psychology at the University of Toronto. Bott submitted five names, these individuals were interviewed, and Cosgrave was offered the position. Over the next four years, he built a staff of five; developed a number of selection tests of ability, achievement, and personality; and undertook research to assist department managers with their human-relations problems.

THE EARLY YEARS

There is no recorded history of industrial/organizational (I/O) psychology in Canada. [*Editors' note: Some of the material in this chapter was published as an article (Webster, 1988) in a special issue of Canadian Psychologist devoted to*

I/O psychology (Catano & Tivendell, 1988)]. Journal articles and the Canadian Psychological Association (CPA) Archives include a few one-sentence mentions; that is all. This account that follows is based on my own recollections and information supplied by Dr. Gerald P. Cosgrave and Mr. John B. Boyd. "The Early Years" refers to the period ending with the publication of the CPA Directory in February 1946. This is really the story of six personnel psychologists and the major problems they encountered.

DR. GERALD P. COSGRAVE

Cosgrave's initial appointment draws attention to one problem that haunted the profession throughout its history: that of *identity*. Employed because he was a psychologist, this word was not part of his title, and in fact, many in management did not realize his background until his name began to appear in newspaper interviews and reports. This non-recognition of the designation "psychologist" was to be the rule rather than the exception.

Speaking personally, I was assured in the mid-1930s, I would have a contract with a major corporation if I would cease calling myself a psychologist. John Boyd, as will be shown, was employed by the Robert Simpson Company in 1937 because of his training and experience as a psychologist. He was advised not to make this public and, in fact, to keep quiet that he was even a university graduate. One Montreal-based corporation employed a psychologist as a "psychologist" in the mid-1950s, but he discovered that salary increases would be few and far between until he accepted a more suitable title. He became an academic. A number of McGill graduates were employed during the 1950s and 1960s by Montreal firms; not one had the word "psychologist" in his title. Most ceased to think of themselves as personnel psychologists and identified instead with the personnel management profession. The word "psychologist" does not appear in the job titles of a single personnel psychologist employed by government or industry and listed in the CPA Directory of 1946 or 1956. The word was applied to many clinicians in hospitals and to a number of school psychologists. How do we maintain our identity?

Cosgrave returned to the University of Toronto in 1932 and was on the academic staff for eleven years. Vocational and industrial psychology was among the subjects taught. He left the department in 1943 to establish a vocational counselling service for the Toronto YMCA. This was the first community educational vocational guidance service in Ontario and probably the first in Canada. The balance of his professional life was devoted to vocational counselling, and in 1972, this was recognized by honorary doctorate degrees from York University and from Université Laval.

This brief personal account of one psychologist's professional history illustrates a second major problem that faced the profession: the *role* of the industrial psychologist.

The profession originated in the United States immediately after World War I, when many ex-personnel army officers transferred their skills in the classification of recruits by means of psychological test scores to the selection of plant, office, and sales staff. It was then regarded as self-evident that if these tests could predict job success of applicants, they would be of equivalent value when used to advise young people on the choice of a career. The sub-specialty of vocational guidance developed as part of the normal function of an industrial personnel psychologist. This role has continued, although, by the late 1960s, the concept of counselling had broadened considerably.

The social psychology experiments at the Hawthorne plant of Western Electric provided the foundation for organizational psychology. No Canadian interest was shown in these studies until after the war, when a few practitioners became interested in leadership behaviour and productivity changes through group processes. This new role is reflected in the job title of only one industrial psychologist listed in the 1956 CPA Membership Directory. It was late in the 1960s when "organizational" became hyphenated with "industrial" as a professional specialty.

Two more Toronto graduates are included in this pre-World War II account.

MR. JOHN B. BOYD

John B. Boyd, BA from Toronto (1929), MA from Toronto (1932), was one of the first group of Toronto psychology graduates to be trained (1929) for work in the Ontario Mental Health Clinics. Somewhat bored and frustrated with the direction his career had taken, he wrote the president of the Robert Simpson Company and suggested they could use an industrial psychologist. He was employed in 1937 as assistant employment manager and was assured he could work in his free time on such things as validating tests. There was little spare time, and probably he would have resigned, except he was invited to enter the Army Directorate of Personnel Selection.

After the war, he returned to Simpsons with the rank of special assistant to the general superintendent and this did provide an opportunity to be a personnel psychologist. A better opportunity appeared in 1952, when he joined Ontario Hydro as supervisor of Personnel Research—a position he held until retirement 20 years later.

MR. KENNETH COX

Kenneth Cox, BSc from Toronto (1931), MA from Boston (1932), is advanced here with a slight reservation, even though he was a personnel industrial psychologist from about 1933. Located in Hamilton, he specialized in vocational guidance for a number of years and then moved into a broader personnel psychology field.

Cox is an excellent example of a self-trained psychologist who was fully accepted. He represents a third major problem area: *training*. His Toronto degree was not in psychology, and the one from Boston almost certainly was not, although, I am told, it was intended to produce professionals in vocational guidance.

No Canadian university in the pre-World War II period produced graduates intended specifically to be professionals. All professionals were self-trained, and it would be most unfair to reject intelligent, self-educated persons of high ethical standards simply because their degrees are not adequate in terms of the 1980s. It should be remembered that 20% of CPA members in the 1946 directory listed the BA as their highest degree. This included four of the fourteen industrial psychology members (one other is known not to have had any degree).

PRE-WAR PROFESSIONAL PRACTICE

McGill is the other university that produced personnel psychologists prior to World War II. It accepted research funds in 1931 to participate in research on employment and related subjects. As discussed earlier in Chapter 2, this enabled me to spend the summer of 1933 as an intern in vocational guidance with the National Institute of Industrial Psychology in London, England; to operate a free vocational guidance clinic for high school graduates in the summer of 1934; and to open my own office as a consulting psychologist in vocational guidance in 1935. Financially this office was a failure, but as discussed previously, it led to the establishment in 1936 of the Psychological Institute, incorporated by Bois and myself, both 1936 PhDs from McGill, to provide public education and professional services to individuals and business organizations.

The McGill Department of Psychology gave 100% support, and within a year, the Psychological Institute was responsible for the administration of a good part of the Youth Training Plan in Quebec. We recommended training programmes; undertook psychological assessment of young people; determined who would receive trade or on-the-job training; and were responsible for job placement. In 1938, personnel evaluations for companies became an important part of our activity, and we expanded into consumer market research and public measurement through a federally chartered firm, Opinion Surveys Limited.

ONSET OF THE WAR

Personnel psychology was developing well until the Army became interested in personnel selection. Bois was the only French-Canadian psychologist with any expertise in this area, and we believed he had to accept a commission when a directorate was established. A major undertaking in early 1942 was a survey of morale among army troops. This contributed to the formation of the Directorate of Special Services, designed, in part, to keep headquarters aware of morale and conditions affecting this. In mid-1942, I accepted a commission to join the directorate and study morale. As noted earlier, arrangements to ensure the continuation of the Psychological Institute and Opinion Surveys Limited proved unsatisfactory, and both charters were surrendered.

One civilian who entered the Canadian picture during the war deserves mention: Dr. Herbert Moore. Moore was a Newfoundlander by birth, receiving a BA from Toronto (1924) and a PhD from Harvard. He was brought to Canada in about 1943 by Mr. Paul Kellogg, president of Stevenson and Kellogg, Management Engineers, to provide psychological assessments for both individuals and companies. The 1946 CPA Directory establishes that Moore had working with him at least five psychologists, located in Toronto, Montreal, and Vancouver. Over the following ten years, this firm provided valuable experience and practical training to a number of personnel psychologists who went on to establish their own consulting firms.

THE POST-WAR PERIOD FOR I/O PSYCHOLOGY

Chapter 4 focuses on aspects of personnel psychology during the war years, Chapter 5 on professional training, and Chapter 6 on the impact of the Canadian Psychological Association on the development of professional psychology. The present section is an initial overview of the post-war history of professional psychology, with a particular focus on industrial/organizational psychology.

This initial overview begins with the February 1946 CPA Membership Directory and concludes in 1965, with the aftermath of the Couchiching Conference on professional psychology. There is little solid information on what took place during this 20-year period. Neither early journals nor the CPA Archives say anything substantial. The only revealing information comes from a comparison of CPA industrial and clinical members.

By the mid-1940s, non-academic members of the CPA were becoming negative. They believed the association was overly dominated by academics with no interest in professionals. Specifically, they wanted the CPA to certify professionals and to improve training. The British North America Act does not permit federal corporations to control professionals, and so dissatisfaction continued to grow. Some non-academics resigned; many professionals did not join the CPA.

Bois returned to private practice as an industrial psychologist and sought the presidency of the CPA in an effort to strengthen the role of the professional. He was the first (1949) of only three non-academic presidents from 1938 to 1965. His conclusion was that provincial associations should be encouraged. He left both psychology and Canada by 1960.

Professionals, whatever their specialty, were dissatisfied. Therefore, we can trace I/O history to some extent by comparing CPA membership by clinical psychologists and industrial psychologists.

The 1946 CPA Directory contains 238 names, including 14 in industrial psychology positions and seven in clinical positions. In addition, there were 67 in military service; some of these moved in as personnel psychologists; others as clinical psychologists. Membership in the CPA increased to 746 by 1956, and this included 49 in industrial and 93 in clinical positions. There were almost twice as many clinical as industrial psychologists—a complete reversal from the 1946 situation. Casual examination of the 1967 CPA Directory suggests that the discrepancy between the two areas of specialization increased in this second ten-year period. Examination of the 1956 membership list reveals interesting differences between the specialties.

Industrial psychologists were concentrated in Ontario and Quebec (80%), while clinicians were found in every province, with little more than half in the two central ones. While not a single employed industrial psychologist had the word "psychologist" in his title, almost every clinician did. There were no women industrial psychologists. Private practice through consulting firms accounted for about one third of the I/O psychologists but for only two clinicians. Why did I/O psychologist fall behind? Four situations contributed:

1. Lacking the word "psychologist" in job titles, some individuals identified with other occupation groups, for example, personnel associations.

2. No financial support was available for I/O students, while, by 1948, clinical candidates could receive substantial mental health bursaries.

3. I/O training programmes had no government support, whereas mental health funds were available to pay salaries of clinical academics. Mooney (1963) reported nine universities had clinical training; only two (McGill and Université de Montréal) had industrial programmes,

although graduates from other universities with general training entered the I/O area.

4. MBA graduates with I/O training were preferred to psychology graduates because they were seen to be more mobile within the organization.

The influence of these conditions can be illustrated through the McGill experience with a two-year non-thesis master's programme that produced 129 graduates in either vocational-industrial or clinical psychology between 1950 and 1970. At least 45 went on to a doctorate. Only 25 followed the vocational-industrial option. A 1982 follow-up of McGill graduates indicated:

1. Most clinicians had the word "psychologist" in their job title, but not a single graduate working for a company had this. More important, not one considered himself to be a psychologist (as noted earlier, there were no women industrial psychologists); each was identified as being a personnel or other manager.

2. The department budget had to meet all costs of the vocational-industrial programme, and there was no funding available for student support. Not only did mental health grants pay the salaries of clinical professors, but they provided excellent bursaries for Canadian students. Motivation had to be high to follow the vocational-industrial route, yet graduates did not remain "psychologists."

3. Most members of the McGill Department of Psychology never accepted the idea of professional training. Some may have been guided by principle, but for others, it was finances. As discussed in Chapter 5, it was necessary in 1952 to establish a semi-autonomous Applied Psychology Centre to administer the budget and ensure the continuation of professional activities.

4. Several of the companies with which we worked closely were suggesting, by the early 1960s, that MBA graduates with I/O studies would be more mobile within the firm than our graduates.

At the 1965 Couchiching Conference on Professional Psychology, discussed further in Chapters 1 and 6, there were few mentions of I/O psychology; clinicians held the floor. As editor of the proceedings (Webster, 1967), my conclusion was that development depended upon new sources of money being discovered. An unlocated protest by Dr. Virginia Douglas a year or two after Couchiching criticized the CPA Board for "dragging its heels" over implementation of conference recommendations, including this one.

Thus was launched the modern era of professional psychology in Canada, including I/O psychology. How that era evolves in the future will require another story by another participant-observer.

CHAPTER 4

PSYCHOLOGY AND THE CANADIAN ARMY DURING THE WAR YEARS:

1939–1945

WORK OF CANADIAN PSYCHOLOGISTS IN RELATION to the war effort is *not* an example of professional psychology, but these years and this effort, as have been described by Vipond and Richert (1977), are important for their effect on the profession. Many Canadian psychologists made significant contributions that have been overlooked or downplayed. One in particular deserves to be selected for special mention: Professor E. A. Bott, *de facto* chairman of the Department of Psychology at the University of Toronto from the very early 1920s and actual chairman from 1926 to 1956. He above anyone else deserves special credit for the fact psychologists were permitted to apply personnel selection methods in the war years between 1942 and 1945. He made other contributions, as will be seen. Also, he deserves credit for the fact that at least half of all psychologists directly involved in the Canadian war effort were staff members or graduates of his department at the University of Toronto. Nothing I have read in journal articles prepared me for these contributions.

THE INFLUENCE OF PROFESSOR E. A. BOTT
AND THE UNIVERSITY OF TORONTO

Professor E. A. Bott, as we will see in Chapter 6, was the leading spirit behind the founding of the Canadian Psychological Association (CPA) for the specific purpose of involving psychologists when war was declared. He saw the need for a national association to deal with government. How right he was! As Bois and I found, individuals could make no impression. Recognizing the approach of war and evaluating our professional activities, we made two approaches to the federal government as alluded to earlier; both failed miserably. To briefly recount these approaches:

- Based on our work described earlier on selecting and placing unemployed youth registered with the Youth Training Plan in Quebec, documentation was submitted to the minister of National Defence in July or August 1939. We believed psychologists could contribute significantly to the selection and allocation of personnel. A reply was received within a week or ten days. It was short. It said, in effect, that the minister had every confidence that his officers had both the experience and the knowledge of how recruits should be selected and placed, and he was assured outsiders could not contribute positively. That ended that effort. Bott was correct; a national body would be required.

- Opinion Surveys Limited had a network of interviewers across the country and had demonstrated the value of opinion polls. A month or two before hostilities began, a group of media and public relations personnel got together with me, and we prepared a proposal to organize a public information service for Canada based on our opinion polls. This was submitted to cabinet through a senior minister. We were invited to a meeting with the secretary to the prime minister at seven p.m. on September 2 and were assured our proposal was on the cabinet meeting agenda for that evening. The proposal was rejected. Psychologists never did get far in this field, but our failure is further evidence Bott was correct in his belief that only a national organization could break down strong barriers.

Actually, the University of Toronto Department of Psychology became actively involved with the war effort early in 1939, after Dr. Brock Chisholm, a RCAF psychiatrist at the time, visited Professor Bott, expressed his certainty that war was near, and convinced Bott he should review all relevant research. Gerald Cosgrave was assigned this task that he completed by the September outbreak of war.

Things moved very rapidly. An associate committee on Aviation Medical Research was established in the department, with E. A. Bott as director; and Gerald Cosgrave as supervisor and, in Bott's absence, director. Two young psychologists—B. M. Springbett, MA, and R. L. W. Ritchie, BA—comprised junior staff. This group examined, developed, and did validation research on a number of tests, including measures of alertness, steadiness, stereoptic vision, serial reaction times, two-hand coordination, and night-vision intensity. It also worked on an aviation aptitude test, a trade aptitude examination, an air cadet aptitude test, and a 30-minute interview format.

It will be seen shortly that on October 2, 1939, a conference on the use of psychological methods in warfare was held in Ottawa under the auspices of the National Research Council. Plans for the work described above were sufficiently far along that this effort received considerable attention.

The CPA was swift to react when war was declared on September 3, 1939. The very next day several members met at the University of Toronto to discuss our possible contribution. They convened a special CPA meeting at Queen's University on September 11 that discussed where our war effort could best be directed: Personnel selection or morale problems in the armed forces? Selection of workers in the war industry? Formulation of propaganda and the operation of psychological warfare? Obviously, these academics believed their science could be applied successfully over a wide range of activities.

EARLY DEVELOPMENTS TOWARDS PSYCHOLOGY'S CONTRIBUTIONS

The meeting decided to devise a set of psychological tests that could be offered without cost to the military. In this, they were influenced by the presence of

Chester Kellogg and N. Whitman Morton, both associate professors at the McGill Department of Psychology. They had developed a civilian version of the non-verbal intelligence Army (US) Beta test on which Professor Kellogg had worked during World War I.

Professor Morton was appointed chairman of a committee to proceed immediately with the construction of such a test, and Professor Liddy's committee, set up in April 1939, went out to raise funds. Before this meeting ended, the principal of Queen's University offered to bring the whole matter before the National Research Council.

Only three weeks later, October 2, 1939, a conference on the use of psychological methods in wartime was convened by the National Research Council in Ottawa under the chairmanship of Sir Frederick Banting. The Navy, Army, and Air Force were represented, as was the CPA and the Associate Committee on Aviation Medical Research; moreover, Major General A. G. L. McNaughton, president of National Research Council, was present.

There was considerable discussion about research underway at the University of Toronto on the selection of Air Force pilots, but interest centred on the use of psychological tests in the classification of personnel. General McNaughton was favourably disposed but wanted evidence of their practical value. According to Carver (1945), who did not provide a source for the quotation, the conference decided "that it would be advisable to introduce into the recruiting examinations, intelligence and aptitude tests and supplementary trade tests, and that advantage should be taken of the offer of the Canadian Psychological Association to assist in the development and institution of these tests and to this end the Director General of Medical Services should be asked to cooperate with a committee appointed by this conference" (pp. 6-7). The committee was comprised of three psychologists, an army neurosurgeon, and an army officer, and its mandate was to carry forward these recommendations. As Carver (1945) went on the comment, "the significance of this Conference lay in the fact that Canada's senior scientific body had placed a stamp of approval upon the project of the little group of psychologists" (p. 7).

It was assumed that all three services might use the same system, but no representative of either the Navy or Air Force had been named to the committee and both services withdrew from the efforts of the CPA. Shortly after the meeting, General McNaughton went overseas and the Army lost most of its interest.

The CPA proceeded to develop an aptitude "M" test under the direction of N. W. Morton. Members volunteered time and effort to prepare draft forms of 12 subtests, to administer and score tests, to undertake small experiments, to analyze results, and to revise the examination. All had full-time positions, and volunteering meant evening and weekend work. Morton made the test development as simple as possible. The first printed version was available in February 1940. As Wright (1974) quite correctly noted, "The story of these early years is an inspiring example of dedicated, cooperative effort" (p. 116). As we return to later, the same cannot be said of another story.

Volunteer CPA members administered the test to more than 1000 soldiers in March 1940. Officers provided ratings of each man's ability on a simple rating scale. Results were fed back to unit officers, and they were satisfied the tests might have some value. So too were officers in units where test scores were used to recommend promotion to the rank of corporal or lance corporal. While the military were satisfied, nothing was done for a year or more. Testing procedures were the responsibility of no one.

E. A. Bott in Toronto and G. Humphrey of Queen's persevered, and in January 1941, commanding officers were informed that trained psychologists were available to test units of 50 personnel or more of all ranks. Thirty psychologists, including 14 university professors, 7 school inspectors, 4 teachers, and 5 full-time research workers, had volunteered. They tested almost 10,000 army personnel of ranks up to and including major. Morton's committee and volunteers scored tests and analyzed material. Results indicated the test was valuable in predicting who should be upgraded, but it did not help distribute personnel among the various arms and trades.

The Army was not overly impressed. It requested the CPA develop a test of mechanical aptitude; the CPA agreed and then the Army decided to rely on American materials. There is no telling what might have happened if the decision had been otherwise.

At this point in time, General McNaughton, responsible for the Canadian Army overseas, demanded the establishment of a personnel selection branch in Canada. Carver (1945) wrote that McNaughton and the senior officers had come to the view that "a dangerous proportion of men who, on account of mental incapacity and emotional instability, had been unable to meet the stress of training and the strangeness of life in the Army" (p. 32). This was during the early years of the war while the Army was simply on the defensive. As the Army prepared for a more offensive role, McNaughton, as we will see, proceeded to establish a personnel section overseas.

THE PERSONNEL SELECTION BRANCH IN CANADA

[*Editors' note: In November 1986, the directorate of the History of the National Defence Headquarters in Ottawa declassified a 28-page report that had been prepared internally (as Report 164) by Capt. J.M. Hitsman in November 1946, entitled "The Problem of Selection and Reallocation of Personnel in the Canadian Army Overseas, 1939–1946." The report (Hitsman, 1946) appears well documented, the principal sources being "Canadian Military Headquarters' files and certain war diaries and files in the possession of OIC War Diaries, Historical Section, C.M.H.Q" (p. 1). It is available in the National Library and Archives.*

By late 1986, Edward Webster's health had deteriorated to the point where he was not in a position to have become aware of this recently declassified report, or if he had become aware of it, to incorporate its contents into his manuscript or notes.

A second report, to which we have already encountered references in this chapter, is a work by Major H. S. M. Carver (1902–1995) entitled "Personnel Selection in the Canadian Army: A descriptive study" (Carver, 1945). Available through the National Library and Archives, this is not an "official report," although it was published informally in 1945 under the auspices of the Directorate of Personnel Selection, National Defence Headquarters, and its two directors during the war years, Colonel Brock Chisholm, 1941–1942, and Colonel William Line, 1942–1946. Much of the report is Carver's personal account of the war years, parts of which represent a treasure-trove of detailed information on the methods of psychological testing and assessment developed for the Army. It appears as if Vipond and Richert (1977) were not aware of this Carver report in their discussions of psychology in the war years, but Edward Webster appears to have been aware of it and drew upon it in this account. In the sections that follow, the editors have in places added comments based largely on material from these reports, material which complements or augments what Edward Webster wrote.

Before the war, Carver worked in what was to be known as landscape architecture and taught in the Faculty of Architecture of the University of Toronto. After the war, he went on to be influential in community planning and housing, landscape architecture, and in various roles in the Canada Mortgage and Housing Corporation. During the war, between 1942 and 1946, he worked as an army examiner involved in recruitment and personnel selection. As evidenced in his two publications (Carver, 1945, 1975), he had great respect for and was very much influenced by Colonel Line and Colonel Chisholm, who were referred to earlier. This influence becomes evident in Carver's contrasting evaluative discussions of the Personnel Selection Branch in Canada and of Personnel Selection Overseas.]

Professor Bott visited England in the early summer of 1941 and returned to Canada at the end of July. By August 4, an outline had been prepared for building a personnel selection organization consisting of army examiners with training in psychology. The minister of National Defence authorized establishment of the Directorate of Personnel Selection on September 18, 1941. He stated its primary object "is the evaluation of personality and the testing, psychologically, of personnel entering into and already enlisted in the Canadian Army with a view to guiding personnel into positions for which they are best suited as well as advising on the selection of officers and other ranks to fill the varied types of appointment in the Canadian Army" (cited by Carver, 1945, p. 36).

The first director of the Personnel Selection Branch, 1941–42, was Colonel Brock Chisholm, who had been a psychiatrist in civilian life. He had risen in the ranks during the World War I from private to company commander, had been active in the militia between wars, and had entered active service early in 1940. He was quickly upgraded to director general of Medical Services and, by the end of the war, had become a major general and the deputy minister of Health and Welfare for the Dominion of Canada.

He was succeeded in 1942–46 by Colonel William Line, who, before and after the war, was a professor of psychology at the University of Toronto. He had also served in World War I and had been active in the militia. Selection of field staff produced problems, but of the first 50 officers who completed three years of service, 46 had university degrees, including 11 with PhDs. Thirty had been teachers in universities or schools.

From here on, we had a military operation controlled by psychologists, but one of its senior staff members who, before and after the war, was an academic with no interest in applied matters told C. R. Myers while being interviewed for the *Oral History of Psychology in Canada* project, "I didn't see much psychology."

MAJOR JAMES HOWARD
AND PERSONNEL SELECTION OVERSEAS, 1942–1944

General McNaughton did not wait for the Directorate of Personnel Selection to be established before having established separately the Personnel Selection Overseas group. He arranged that Major James Howard (1899–1987) proceed overseas in December 1941 to work on pressing selection problems. The priority task was to locate, among 200,000 troops, individuals with specific skills and qualifications that were required immediately.

Howard's background was excellent. Before the war, he was a Canadian clinical-educational PhD from Cornell University, working in Belleville schools as a teacher and counsellor. He had served in the Royal Flying Corps near the end of World War I and expected a second war with Germany. During his years in Belleville, he was not only active in the militia but went to all available army courses. By May 1940, he was a staff officer at National Defence Headquarters in Ottawa and his duties included working with the CPA on the administration of the "M" test to troops. He could not have had better credentials for his overseas responsibilities.

The problems facing Howard, as Carver (1945) quite aptly agreed, were entirely different from those that faced personnel selection in Canada. In Canada, the prime task was to classify recruits as to where they could best absorb training and be effective. Overseas, it was concerned more with specific skills; for example, if a railroad unit was required, who, among the 200,000 soldiers, could fill the 30 different job classifications?

The monograph prepared by Carver (1945) outlined quite objectively much of what was done between 1942 and 1944 but was very negative in its evaluation. Carver saw no excuse for the highly centralized organization that, as he characterized it, put cards through a sorter and then notified commanding officers that certain personnel were to be transferred. Howard is accused of creating bad relations with commanding officers, the men transferred, and other unit officers, and with undermining the effectiveness of his own field officers as advisors.

Study of a detailed unpublished memorandum and accompanying documents prepared by Howard (1943) under circumstances to be outlined in what follows convinces me he would agree with the statements in Carver's report but not with their evaluation. In Howard's view, the need to use men effectively now overrode niceties of feelings. Howard would not worry about a commanding officer's feelings when an effective person was transferred to a place where he was needed more. Nor would Howard have worried the least about the upset to a unit officer when his cooperative, effective "batman" [*Editors' note: a personal "servant" to a commissioned officer, particularly in the British military*] was moved to the Pioneer Corps, where he would be of some value to the Army.

[*Editors' note: An important part of the responsibilities of Personnel Selection Overseas was to identify personnel who could not fit into regular service for reasons of low intelligence, lack of education, mental instability, psychiatric issues, and so on, but who could be assigned to the Pioneer Corps. "The duties assigned these men included the construction of gun pits, the sand-bagging of buildings, landscaping, loading and unloading supplies, road-building and excavation, salvage, fatigues and maintenance" (Hitsman, 1946, p. 12–13).*]

The decisions on how to organize this chapter on the war years were almost made when, in 1984, Dr. Howard shared with me a lengthy memorandum with multiple appendices he had prepared in October 1943 to describe and justify to headquarters in Ottawa the approach and actions of his group overseas. I was impressed by this document, both its content as well as the detail provided. I became fully convinced of its significance for this chapter when I read the *Oral History Interview* between C. R. Myers and W. R. Blair. (Dr. Blair has reviewed this chapter and in personal correspondence on March 18, 1985, approved the use of the quotes and attributions that follow). At the time of the interview, Dr. Blair was professor of psychology and chairman of the department at the University of Calgary. He had obtained a degree and teacher status in 1937 and had hoped to become a psychologist. He enlisted early in the war as a gunner and won his commission as an officer overseas. He applied for transfer to personnel selection and was accepted without training. Much later, in 1966, while director of Personnel Selection in the Army and president of the Canadian Psychological Association, he became the first director to hold the rank of colonel. In his *Oral History* interview, Blair talked with Myers about many things, but when conversation got around to the Ottawa–London split, he said,

> The Overseas group under Jim Howard I thought did a yeoman service and should not have been criticized for what they were doing. Circumstances dictated that they proceed the way they did. However, this was never understood by the group in Canada, and almost a war went on between the two of them, and they would dispatch delegations and emissaries to go over and put things right.

THE MAKINGS OF A "WAR" WITHIN THE WAR

What Howard had done, as he had been instructed to do by his chief of staff, was to categorize the Canadian Army Overseas:

- to determine who should be there and who should be returned to Canada as unfit for the field;
- to sort out those who should not be in positions where they were;
- to get them into positions that would better suit their abilities; and
- to begin to identify those who were capable of being upgraded as non-commissioned officers and even as officers.

It was a massive sorting problem that had to be conducted. You couldn't do this, as Howard perceived it, using interviews and individual-type testing, and so he undertook a mass programme of classification, making use of information that had been gathered in Canada, the "M" test score, for example, and records of education and previous civilian experience. Together with ratings of performance judged by unit officers overseas, he used a machine card system (Hollerith system) to sort people out; at least that was the objective. Blair pointed out that machine card sorting had its drawbacks—for example, it was often out of date. Apparently, there was a big snafu over selection of personnel for Forestry Corps, but I was unable to find out more about that.

This approach was contrary to the clinically oriented approach that William Line had adopted in Canada and that, as described earlier, involved primarily an individual interview that was the central and essential part of selection and classification. Blair went on to describe what was happening in Canada, where personnel selection officers were "poor-men's psychiatrists, clinically oriented but unqualified clinicians."

[*Editors' note: In his autobiography, Carver (1975) included, as follows, a description of the personnel selection approach taken in Canada:*

> *Under Brock Chisholm and Bill Line, two men of independent and humanitarian spirit, there was no risk that the system would become a cold psychometric machine for sorting out men like mice in the laboratory. The real essence of their system was the patient clinical interview to discover the 'whole man' and the environment in which he had grown and the influences to which he had responded.*

> *I became one of Bill Line's team when the system was finally put into operation at the beginning of 1942 and for the next four years this was my whole life. I talked with thousands of young Canadians in a kind of confessional relationship that could only occur in wartime when career decisions are fateful. I discovered that there are no stereotypes: each man who told me about himself and his aspirations was a lonely individual, trying to understand himself and the world around him (p. 62).*]

According to my correspondence with Blair (personal correspondence, W. R. N. Blair, March 18, 1985), the conflict between Line and Howard became "vicious."

[*Editors' note: In his memoir of the war years, George Ferguson (1992) comments on the significant philosophical and ideological differences between the Directorate of Personnel Services in Ottawa, headed directly by Line and indirectly by Chisholm, and Personnel Selection Overseas, headed by Howard. Political/ professional manoeuvring is also evident in Ferguson's discussion of efforts, ultimately unsuccessful, to have all personnel selection services made part of the Royal Canadian Army Medical Corps, headed by Chisholm.*]

Howard, according to Blair, lost out to Line, the director in Ottawa, because Line was a most convincing speaker: "Line could mesmerize people when he talked." As Blair commented in the 1985 letter, referenced above, to me: "He [Line] was completely committed to the idea that individuals must be protected from becoming mere ciphers even in an authoritarian organization. The army examiners exposed to his philosophy in Canada approached their overseas assignments, with Howard, like missionaries bent on converting the selection system and people to their way of thinking."

This evaluation by Blair, a man who had spent more than 20 post-war years successfully in the Canadian Army Personnel Selection organization, places Howard in a position much different from how he has been portrayed. Because so little is on public record of the aspirations and achievements of this clinical-educational psychologist, fairly copious extracts from the memorandum and supporting documents Howard prepared in his defence (Howard, 1943) are summarized for the record in what follows. I have also drawn upon personal correspondence with Howard (1984) available through the National Archives.

WHAT WAS REALLY GOING ON?

APPROACH OF PERSONNEL SELECTION OVERSEAS

It should be noted that by early 1943, Personnel Selection Overseas had a staff of 72 officers, who, with their assistants, had tested, interviewed, and prepared documentation on all 200,000 Canadian Army personnel. They had had to fill some 59 job classifications. To use the example outlined earlier, if a unit of railway troops was required, this called for locating soldiers with civilian experience and competence in some 30 different jobs. In addition, there were other tasks such as locating low caliber men, likely to create problems, and placing them in the Pioneer Corps.

Howard's conception of selection policy involved the broadest possible psychological basis for the behaviour of the individual solider within the Army. Its purpose was to ensure the maximum utilization of the individual soldier's talents within and for the Army. This involved a qualitative as well as a quantitative evaluation of manpower.

The salient principle underlying selection policy was the attainment of maximum economy in the employment of available manpower. This has many implications. To quote from Howard's memorandum:

a) . . . it is essential that large numbers of personnel be available who are thoroughly trained in and have a knowledge of technical military equipment and who are capable of functioning satisfactorily in a highly complex organization. If such personnel are to be made available in sufficient numbers, a careful investigation must be made into each soldier's qualifications in order to ensure a minimum wastage of talent results. . . .

b) A modern army is a developmental organization with constantly changing requirements. This necessitates a machinery capable of locating rapidly personnel with specialist qualifications. . . . To locate personnel with specialist qualifications to satisfy any such contingency is a primary function of selection work.

c) The limitations of available Canadian manpower and the competing demands of Navy, Air Force, and industry . . . render early recognition of the individual soldier's abilities and the application of such abilities to army requirements a highly essential task. . . .

d) Economy of time in training military personnel is highly desirable under existing conditions. . . . Advising training officers in the abilities of soldiers under their command is a feature of selection work which is essential in making the best use of time and manpower. (Howard, 1943, p. 1–2)

Howard appreciated a second important principle underlying selection policy: the recognition of certain psychological needs of the individual, and their satisfaction within the limitations allowed by the system of employment within the army. He went on to discuss the effect on military careers of such things as the need for security, utilization of civilian skills acquired at considerable expense and effort, adjustments to the military environment, and the desirability of continuity and progress.

There is little if anything in these statements that the Ottawa headquarters would dispute. It was Howard's method of implementation that created the problem. It is my personal belief that what Howard did would have been approved by most of the leading post-war industrial psychologists.

DETAILS OF PERSONNEL SELECTION OVERSEAS PROCEDURES

What follows is essentially a condensation of Howard's (1943) description of his personnel selection procedures:

Howard, a clinician, believed, as have post-war industrial psychologists, that good selection involves careful description of individuals, careful description of the environment in which they may be called upon to operate, and the relating of the individual to the environment to ensure a maximum likelihood of efficient performance. Applying this concept to the military front in England, Howard looked at the procedures for describing the soldier, his employment, and his relations to the army job. His way of describing the individual soldier is of greatest interest to the professional psychologist.

While Personnel Selection Overseas administered Revised Test "M," a number of other aptitude and personality tests were also applied. These included examinations commonly used in the American and British Army—but they went beyond these. In addition, an individual interview was held with each soldier. Its content was similar to that of most interviews recommended for selection and placement purposes in industry.

All information was recorded on a qualification card that was maintained at headquarters as Howard had quickly found that army record organization did not permit the existence of a personnel selection record that would accompany the soldier. Nor was it practical to have sufficient officers attached to units to maintain records.

It was essential to develop a system capable of quickly furnishing information regarding specialized skills, technical qualifications, and potentialities. This ruled out a highly decentralized documentary system but did justify the establishment of qualification (Q) cards for overseas personnel maintained centrally. The card was designed to facilitate filing, indexing, availability of individual items, coding, and so on, without detracting from its use to obtain a completely integrated description of the soldier and his employment possibilities. Almost 200,000 men had to be tested and interviewed in order to complete this Q card. The field staff had little training or experience in interviewing. These conditions necessitated a simple record that could be completed in a minimum of time. Also, the card should be compatible with the records maintained by the British and American personnel selection organizations in the United Kingdom. In addition, material would have to be transferred to a mechanical card sorting system that could readily locate personnel with specific qualifications.

This Q card that appears to have been a central issue in the dispute within personnel selection between Ottawa and London deserves a brief description.

Printed on both sides, the card measured 14 inches by 10 inches, and it covered some 48 areas of background, civilian and military, that ranged from home life and education through hobbies and interests to post-war expectations, as well, of course, as providing a physical and mental description. Arranged for easy recording of facts, it permitted interviewer comments and remarks. A 15-page, legal size, and single-spaced manual was required to describe how to complete the form. Obviously, it could not be sorted readily and so the factual information was transferred to cards designed for machine sorting. Each man required three cards.

Howard believed that interviews undertaken to obtain Q-card information were as "clinical" as the competency of the interviewer would permit. The fact information is transferred to a card that will be machine sorted rather than reported in free description cannot, he stated, "be used as an argument against the use of the Q card part of a clinical procedure. The collection of facts is an integral part of the clinical process. The method of recording these facts is not an integral part of the clinical process" (Howard, 1943, appendix 3, p. 2). One experimental comparison of the two methods of reporting is referred to in the report. It showed no substantive differences, although the Q card in most cases was substantially more comprehensive. (No one who supports the use of computer-processed information over "clinical" judgment will dispute Howard's position; Dr. Lee Cronbach ably justified it in 1949.)

Actually, Howard, in 1943, argued that the psychological clinical aspects of personnel selection are liable to meaningless exaggeration. He believed that, judged by professional clinical standards, work both in Canada and overseas was of a low order although usually adequate to meet normal army requirements. He was, however, proud of the clinical methods employed by his group in officer selection; he believed they were more advanced than any used by the Army in Canada.

OFFICER SELECTION

A brief digression to officer selection is justified as Howard appears to have been criticized principally for what was seen as his non-clinical, mechanical-sorting approach to selection. Appendix 16 of the 1943 Memorandum describes officer selection in detail. Howard's procedures not only anticipated the civilian assessment centres developed initially through AT&T in the 1960s and then widely adopted in one form or another, but they provided for better evaluation and more protection of the needs of the candidate.

The officer assessment process required three days: 72 men early in the week, 75 late in the week. A field staff of 12 participated in the evaluation of each group. Personnel officers administered both objective and projective tests, scored and interpreted this material, and conducted the interview. Experienced military officers put candidates through a number of exercises where they worked alone or in groups; certain behaviours were looked for. An education officer checked that each candidate was suitably prepared educationally and technically for what would be expected of him. Any candidate who displayed behaviour that might indicate instability, or the like, was referred for interview to the psychiatrist.

These examining officers reported each candidate to a three-man board (a colonel and two lieutenant colonels), who usually were assisted by two visiting officers representing the Arm of Service to which the candidate belonged. These three to five knowledgeable field officers studied the information collected and had advice from those who had collected it. The three-man board then reached a decision.

I am impressed. After 15 years of research on the employment interview (Webster, 1964, 1982), I am convinced an employment decision is most likely to be accurate when the final decision is made by highly knowledgeable persons with "gut-feelings" about what is needed, working from information not contaminated by personal contact with the applicant. Dr. Howard, the only pre-World War II Canadian professional psychologist with training as a clinician, had brought a clinician approach to the selection of officers. There is no reason to doubt his assertion that his approach to classification and selection among other ranks was as "clinical" as conditions permitted. One must remember that in mid-1942, once Bois had been transferred from Personnel Selection to the Directorate of Special Services, as described in the Closing Comment of this chapter, not a single psychologist on staff in Ottawa was either trained or experienced as a clinician.

REORIENTATION OF PERSONNEL SELECTION OVERSEAS

As noted earlier, Carver was a non-psychologist historian of personnel selection and was a member of the Ottawa headquarters' staff. In civilian life, both before and after the war, he was a well-known and respected architect and urban planner and, for a while, taught architecture at the University of Toronto.

Through his role with the headquarters' staff, Carver was particularly critical of the lack of interest in public relations displayed by Personnel Selection Overseas.

Personnel officers, in both areas, were advisors to commanding officers. In Canada, this meant everything possible was done to create harmonious relations between unit personnel officers and the commander; otherwise, one could not count on the commander wanting advice. To Carver, Howard was continually asking for trouble and undermining his field staff when, from London, orders came from him to transfer personnel.

[Editors' note: The Hitsman (1946) report indicates that compulsory posting and transfer of personnel was highly controversial, and in the end, in April 1943, General McNaughton issued a directive approving the policy. The directive stressed "the immediate necessity for adopting a policy designed to affect the employment of every individual in that capacity for which he is best suited by reason of his physical and mental capacity, his training, and his nature aptitude" (Hitsman, 1946, p. 16). The general went on to say, "I fully appreciate that this policy will to a degree cut across the lines of individual preferences and will affect to some extent the control that an Officer Administering or an Officer Commanding has over personnel of his Corps or Unit. It is inevitable that it will result in the removal from units of men whose loss will be felt. Notwithstanding these disadvantages, however, I am convinced that this action is necessary for the well-being of the army as a whole, and I therefore expect all Commanders loyally to accept my decision and to do all things in their power to facilitate this necessary adjustment" (p. 16). This directive seemingly did not deter Chisholm or Line from continuing to press for Personnel Selection Overseas to come under the Personnel Selection section in Canada, but the material in the report suggests continued skepticism of their efforts. For example, it is reported that in November 1943, Brigadier Booth commented in a memorandum on Line's attitude: "It is clear to me that notwithstanding his several visits to his country, he is still seriously lacking in appreciation of the problems of administering an army in the field" (Hitsman, 1946, p. 23).]

Things came to a head early in 1944 when Ottawa issued direct instructions that Lieutenant-Colonel James Howard was to be removed and replaced by Lieutenant-Colonel N. W. Morton from Canada.

[*Editors' note: According to Hitsman's (1946) report, Lieutenant-Colonel N. W. Morton, who had been part of the Directorate of Personnel Selection in Canada since at least 1942, was dispatched to Britain to transition the leadership of Personnel Selection Overseas from Lieutenant-Colonel Howard. It was agreed formally that Personnel Selection Overseas would "remain distinct but there would be closer liaison between Canada and the United Kingdom and there was to be a greater exchange of officers" (Hitsman, 1946, p. 23). The appointment of Lieutenant-Colonel Morton may have been intended to be temporary because, as noted by Carver (1945, p. 124) and by Hitsman (1946, p. 27), Lieutenant-Colonel R. Wees succeeded Lieutenant-Colonel Morton as AAG(SP) shortly afterwards in June 1944. But there may have been other considerations as well. As requested by his sole source, Edward Webster did not identify Lieutenant-Colonel Morton in the original manuscript as the replacement, but the editors added it to the manuscript since Lieutenant-Colonel Morton had been so identified in Hitsman's (1946) report and in a memoir by Ferguson (1992). Ferguson had worked with Lieutenant-Colonel Howard at the time of the formation of Personnel Selection Overseas, and expressed the opinion that, "J. W. Howard, a man of intelligence, loyalty, and great personal sympathy, was in many ways misunderstood, and unjustly so" (p. 704).*]

The order was implemented and one of the first steps taken to implement integration of Ottawa and London was shredding of documentation, including all machine-sort cards.

[*Editors' note: In his correspondence with Edward Webster, Howard (personal correspondence, J. W. Howard, November 24, 1984; included in Howard, 1984) states that "my 'friends' who took over almost immediately altered my filing system which made it difficult to follow the derailment of my ideas. Also, the punched card system was working well and very efficiently. They destroyed that entire system by shredding the punched cards."*]

I understand the only existing documentation of the Howard era is the copy of the 1943 memorandum and its appendices (several hundred pages) that Dr. Howard kept and loaned to me for this manuscript.

[*Editors' note: Throughout Hitsman's (1946) report are numerous quotations from and references to memoranda, telegrams, and other documentation concerned with personnel selection, but what the report does not contain is consistent with Howard's allegations about shredding and file cleansing. The report, in its entirety, contains virtually no references to any memoranda or reports or telegrams sent by or received by Lieutenant-Colonel Howard, despite the fact he was the senior officer for Personnel Selection Overseas. As well, there is no mention of Lieutenant-Colonel Howard's 1943 memorandum sent to headquarters to explain his approach and the operation of Personnel Selection Overseas. It seems unlikely that in this official history there would be no reference to that memorandum, or to any of the extensive correspondence (Howard, 1946b) between Line and Howard that preceded or followed the preparation of the memorandum, if the memorandum (and other documents) had in fact been in the National Defence files in 1946. The only copy of Howard's (1943) memorandum in the National Archives today is the copy that was deposited privately in 2002 by Dr. Jay Howard, Dr. Howard's son. (That copy happens to include a personal note from Dr. Howard to Edward Webster, written at the time the memorandum was loaned to Edward Webster, and the note includes the allegation of shredding).*]

The British clearly had a different view of Lieutenant-Colonel Howard from that of Ottawa headquarters. Immediately after Lieutenant-Colonel Howard was removed from his role, the British borrowed him for personnel selection duties at the war's end and had him spend several months surveying what was happening in the United States that might be of interest to British Army personnel (Howard, 1946a).

[*Editors' note: According to Hitsman (1946), "Lt.-Col. Howard was loaned to the War Office on 1 Jun 44 to help with the introduction of the PULHEMS System into the British Army. His original four-month attachment kept being extended until 15 Oct 45, when he was repatriated to Canada" (p. 27).*]

According to Dr. Howard, in a letter to me in 1984, "three glowing letters from three British Generals . . . were sent to the Canadian Military Headquarters in London," but on his return to Canada, "the letters had all disappeared." A laudatory letter that recorded Lieutenant-Colonel Howard's work with the British Army in this regard was included in his file.

[*Editors' note: The varied disposition of these letters would suggest, at least as a hypothesis, that the purging of documents related to Lieutenant-Colonel Howard and his work with Personnel Selection Overseas continued beyond the 1944 leadership transition from Lieutenant-Colonel Howard to Lieutenant-Colonel Morton and Lieutenant-Colonel Wees but did end by the conclusion of the war.*]

Canadian psychology has long looked with pride on its contributions to the war effort, and in particular to the application of psychology to personnel selection and allocation. The conflict between psychologists in Ottawa and those in Britain around the appropriate ideological and methodological underpinnings of personnel selection puts something of a cloud over this period of the profession. As a conclusion to this unfortunate saga, let me simply say that, in my opinion, the contribution in England of this Canadian psychologist, James Howard, has been overlooked and neglected, and I hope this review of the situation may facilitate correction and mitigation.

CLOSING COMMENT

I close this chapter with a brief personal anecdote to illustrate the fact personnel selection people in Canada were very sensitive to possible criticism. J. S. A. Bois, one of the first half dozen psychologists (and the first with appropriate professional experiences) brought into the Army specifically for personnel selection, had a minor incident from his background played up on the front page of the nationalist French-language paper *Le Devoir*, in an effort to place the Army in a bad light with Roman Catholics. Quite properly, he was relieved of duties. But when it became clear the *Le Devoir* article was a gross exaggeration and was ignored by all responsible groups, Bois was not reinstated—he was transferred to a new low-profile Directorate of Special Services, as described by Vipond and Richert (1977).

CHAPTER 5

TRAINING PROFESSIONAL PSYCHOLOGISTS

MCGILL UNIVERSITY

THE PRE-PROFESSIONAL PERIOD

AS I HAVE NOTED EARLIER, SEVERAL graduates of McGill became professionals (referred to at that time as "consultants") in the pre-war years, but no professional training was offered until 1949. Dr. Frances Alexander had left the Psychological Institute in about 1943 to become a part-time assistant professor of psychology at McGill. In fact, she carried a heavy teaching load until she left Canada in 1947. She interested several students in clinical careers and had at least two or three MA students who moved into hospital positions. I joined the staff at McGill as special lecturer in January 1946, and in 1947 and 1948 had candidates for the master's degree who sought careers in industrial psychology. Both Alexander's students and mine received comparable training: one or two more or less relevant courses together with a research thesis with a title that sounded vaguely clinical or industrial.

The department was most inadequately staffed for instruction of any kind, undergraduate or graduate, when veterans began to register in 1945 and 1946. The one full-time associate professor and acting chairman, Dr. Chester E. Kellogg, was an ill man; Alexander and I were part-time. The large introductory course was taught by a candidate for the MA. Other MA candidates taught undergraduate courses in 1946 and 1947. A new chairman and professor, Robert MacLeod, arrived in September of 1946, and a year later, he added two full-time staff members: Donald O. Hebb (1904–1985), as a physiological psychologist, and George Ferguson (1914–2001) on the quantitative side. Neither was interested in professional training, although MacLeod's personal interests were more or less applied.

A major change occurred in 1948. Hebb replaced MacLeod as chairman and wanted to establish a mechanism for training professionals. I accepted a position as associate professor, provided I could continue my private practice in personnel selection, guidance, and counselling. Hebb established, on paper, a programme of professional training that attracted five students in the fall of 1949.

EARLY PROFESSIONAL TRAINING

Hebb, by himself, convinced the university to establish two new degrees in psychology: a two-year non-thesis degree (Master of Psychological Science) and a doctorate (Doctor of Psychological Science) with a thesis requirement less rigid than that for the PhD. The master's programme was aimed specifically to produce professionals in clinical, industrial, and counselling psychology. Some might proceed to the new doctorate, but it was designed primarily for persons who had received a research master's but visualized their careers as primarily teaching psychology. The programme would provide students with a much broader base of knowledge than the PhD but would not demand strong research skills.

The professional master's consisted of one academic year of some 12 to 15 hours of courses, and practicums and seminars designed to prepare students for an internship in a hospital, personnel department, or vocational guidance service. Three summer months were spent in full-time internship. This would continue in the same setting two days a week during the second year when additional advanced courses were to be taken and a research report prepared. It should be stressed that the clinical training did not include psychotherapy; the clinician was expected to contribute to diagnosis; and considerable emphasis was placed on testing, both objective and projective. Those in the industrial programme went outside the department for industrial relations courses while those preparing for guidance work went to the Department of Sociology for a course in occupational sociology.

Late in 1948 or early in 1949, the federal government made available mental health funds to establish training in clinical psychology and to assist students who would agree to serve two years in an appropriate clinical setting after graduation. The Department of Psychology received funds to employ one associate professor on a five-year contract, to buy equipment and necessary supplies, and to make available money for student bursaries. Few departments of psychology introduced training programmes, and students who obtained their BA with honours in psychology usually could receive bursaries to McGill. This federal financial assistance continued at least until 1966.

Details of the two new degree programmes had been worked out principally by Hebb and me. Although Ferguson was involved, he had no real interest. Staff were generally uninterested in the new master's programme but reacted very negatively to the one to produce graduates with the Doctorate of Psychological Science (DPsSc) degree: it was nicknamed the "dipsy degree." Three students registered; by the end of the first year, opposition within the department was such that the programme was dropped, and students were invited to transfer to the research-based PhD.

Serious problems soon became evident as a result of the availability of mental health funds at a time when the department was very short of money. It required some years before I realized exactly what was taking place, and no one else seemed to realize what was happening until I drew it to attention.

Simply stated, mental health funds were being diverted to meet department needs. At the very beginning, when the salary for a professor was made available, we agreed it would be excellent if we could locate someone who was not only a good clinical person but could round out the department in another area. We located a highly productive social psychologist who had served as a clinician during and after the war. He was very productive research-wise but was negative to every aspect of clinical training. Excellent reasons were found for diverting other moneys, a little here and a little there, to much needed department equipment or activities.

Staff negativity or indifference to the professional programme tended to create an unhealthy situation, but this might have been overcome in time, except for another situation. Hebb had been largely unknown when he came to McGill in 1947, but by 1950, it was clear he was an outstanding success as an experimental researcher. [*Editors' note: Hebb's book* The Organization of Behavior: A Neuropsychological Theory *continues to influence cognitive neuroscience to this day.*] While much of his work over the years had strong human implications and applications, it was the "pure" laboratory research that was evident in the 1950 period. Hebb and his laboratory provided a "pole" that attracted all staff and students in the research-oriented part of the department, and others were left out in the cold.

By the spring of 1952, I was convinced that the professional programme could not possibly survive, and I resigned from the department. Within a few weeks, Hebb came up with a proposal that promised to create a situation where professionals could survive. I withdrew my resignation; we introduced a structure that produced good professionals for 15 years.

THE APPLIED PSYCHOLOGY CENTRE

Hebb proposed establishment of the Applied Psychology Centre, a semi-autonomous organization within the department that would provide an alternate "pole" to attract and meet the needs of the non-research portion of the department. I was appointed director and geographic professor of psychology. ("Geographic" simply meant that I could use university premises for professional work; a dollar arrangement was agreed upon, and if billings exceeded this, I was giving too much time to outside activities; all such excess income was returned to the department.) This geographic appointment appeared to work well, although I now understand it was resented by some staff and may have contributed to conflict.

The Applied Psychology Centre had its own budget and administered mental health funds. It was responsible for three kinds of activity: professional training; operation of the McGill Guidance Service, a financially self-supporting operation designed primarily for students; and Staff Development Institutes. The institutes were comprised of a series (as many as 12 to 15 a year) of three-day to three-week courses, led by leading American professors, to train personnel and other management people in the community with skills related to industrial/organizational psychology. We can forget the last two services, as, apart from myself, none of the academic staff in the centre or in the department had any interest in either, although Staff Development Institutes provided facilities and equipment of considerable value to both groups.

Professional training was to the master's level only and led to the degree designation "Master of Science Applied, Psychology." (This title had been requested by the graduate faculty, as several departments sought to follow our lead and introduce two-year non-thesis professional degrees. All could use the designation "Master of Science Applied.") It was expected that a few graduates would go beyond the master's to the PhD. They would be in the same research-oriented programme as other PhD candidates, except that one preliminary examination could be in the area of their earlier professional specialty.

The centre's budget provided for full- and part-time staff engaged primarily because of the professional programmes. It was expected that such individuals would also contribute to the department through teaching, committee work, and the direction of PhD candidates, just as department staff would contribute to professional training. One significant difference existed between full-time academics on the centre budget from those on that of the department: The former were expected to hold an outside position related to their professional field and to spend about two days a week in this. I was afraid that, without this professional activity, staff would direct too much of their activity to unrelated research in order to mimic the activity of their department colleagues.

From 1952 until 1966, the centre accepted students who had majored in psychology and sought a master's degree in non-psychotherapy clinical psychology, guidance and counselling, or industrial/organizational psychology. In the early 1960s, an effort was made to develop a specialty to prepare graduates for work in schools, but this proved unacceptable to school authorities who insisted such persons be teachers first, psychologists second. Students were expected to enter professional work on receiving their degree, and those supported by mental health grants—almost every Canadian in the clinical stream—were required by the terms of the grant to work in an appropriate provincial setting for two years.

Mental health funds ensured that the clinical area predominated. Except for two short periods, all full-time academic staff, except myself, were on the clinical side. The first new appointment was Ernest Poser, a graduate of Queen's, who had taken his doctorate in London with Hans Eysenck and had completed two years clinical work in a New Brunswick mental hospital. He was a most fortunate find. While his orientation was clinical, it was such as to be acceptable to most members of the department. As well, his New Brunswick experience enabled him to move into a Montreal mental hospital, and with two days a week, we developed an innovative programme of research as well as of service. Clinical training expanded, and in 1958, mental health funds were increased to provide an assistant professor in addition to Poser, who had entered as an associate professor. Virginia Douglas, a new graduate of the University of Michigan, came on staff with a more psychodynamic orientation sympathetic to traditional psychotherapy. Near the end of the period, a third clinician joined the staff. Montreal hospital psychologists taught and supervised practicums.

No funds were available to support students in the guidance/counselling or industrial/organizational programmes. Students in the guidance/counselling area could receive good field training in local guidance and counselling organizations staffed by psychologists, but those in the industrial stream had to be supervised by personnel managers believed to be intelligent and forward-looking. This was unfortunate; not one of these students, as will be shown, identified with psychology after graduation. Other departments were involved in training non-clinical professionals: Sociology provided a course on occupational behaviour for guidance/counselling candidates; the Industrial Relations Centre broadened the skill basis of those in industrial psychology.

The centre and the department worked well as a team during the six years Hebb was department chairman, and of course, speaking tongue-in-cheek, there were no areas of serious dispute during my six years as chairman. George Ferguson became chairman in 1964, with strong reservations about the desirability of any semi-autonomous group within the department. By this time, it was becoming clear that North America was demanding a doctorate degree for those who wished to be professional psychologists. Once Ontario demanded this, even I recognized that our Master of Science Applied degree could no longer be regarded as adequate preparation for a professional career. Furthermore, by this time, the academic clinicians recognized their unsatisfactory position and were actively striving towards APA approval for a doctorate in clinical psychology based on the scientist-practitioner model. This approval was obtained in 1967.

INTERNAL CONFLICT

In describing training at the Université de Montréal later in this chapter, attention will be drawn to Luc Granger's comments about internal departmental conflict. References to such conflict in departments offering both research and professional training are sufficiently common that it is worth describing this as it appeared at McGill in the 1950s and '60s.

It will be recalled that in the beginning, 1948, Hebb had the idea of separate graduate degrees for students not expected to qualify for research-oriented positions. This was approved, and mental health funds made possible clinical training. I have shown that in the first few years, departmental needs took precedence over those of clinical training, with the result that the Applied Psychology Centre was created. It had a separate budget to halt this diversion of funds. Hebb and I were the only two who welcomed this semi-autonomous organization; most staff were indifferent, and one or two were hostile. This continued over the years.

The centre did act as a buffer to the diversion of both funds and space from professional training. At times, this produced heat. One example will suffice. Centre activities produced university revenue through the Staff Development Institutes, and in consequence, the centre was assigned a building. We only needed two of the three floors and made the third available to the department. Two senior professors assured me the department had need for the whole building. Only the existence of the centre as a formal entity protected use of this space. While the centre could not protect staff and students from derisive remarks about such things as activities off campus, lack of scientific rigour, and purity in research and the like, it could deflect negative action in all but one situation: staff promotion.

The centre, by design, was semi-autonomous. We had not wanted to divorce those preparing professionals from staff working with MA candidates, also centre staff had PhD students who were outside the centre. Therefore, it seemed obvious that promotion should be within the department rather than the centre. This created a very unfortunate situation that penalized full-time academics working in the professional stream and contributed to the demand by clinicians for a professional PhD programme based on the scientist-practitioner model.

Normally the major justification for a department promotion was consensus among senior staff as to the quality of published research. Full-time academic professionals with heavy teaching and supervisory loads plus two days weekly of professional activity had less time for research than did those in the academic research stream; furthermore, they had many fewer students working on research that might be published jointly. Senior department staff did not think highly of research areas of interest to the clinicians. Recognition of this unhealthy restrictive situation undoubtedly fuelled the desire of some clinical staff for a scientist-practitioner model: This would provide a better basis for within-department competition than a practitioner model, which could better prepare students for professional life.

The belief that those in the professional training field were subject to discrimination was fully justified. At a time when it was clear that its days were numbered, the centre secured funds and approval for a promotion. The department held this up for six months while funds were found to give a matching promotion to a non-clinical staff member: "It would not be fair to promote one without the other."

Our experience led me by 1966 to question the viability of professional training within a department with a strong academic research background. The scientist-practitioner compromise may enable the academic to survive, but as Pinard pointed out in 1964, research productivity of such graduates is very limited, and Peterson (1976) has argued they are not as well prepared for professional practice as those trained along practitioner model lines.

THE GRADUATES

Ferguson (1982) suggested that the McGill professional training programme had been minor. Actually, between 1951, when the first professional degree was awarded and 1970 when the last was received, 129 professional degrees were granted compared to 137 MA or MSc degrees—and the last full class of professional master's graduated in 1966.

One would expect major differences between the two groups. After 1950, no one was accepted in the research-oriented programme who was not expected to obtain the PhD in three or four years. The master's year provided training in thesis writing. Occasionally, a student was permitted to proceed to the PhD without receiving the MA or MSc. On the other hand, students were accepted into the professional programme if considered suitable for a terminal master's and had qualifications that appeared to indicate suitability for professional activities.

Actually, there were significant differences between the two groups:

1. Most research students (two-thirds) were male, while the same proportion of professionals was female.

2. The largest numbers of research students came from the United States, with practically none from Canadian universities outside Quebec. (There was good evidence that Canadian universities discouraged better students from applying to McGill.) Most professional students came from Canadian universities, which themselves could provide mental health bursaries to those studying clinical psychology.

3. To prepare a report to the CPA in 1983, I compared the achievements of McGill graduates who obtained the research and professional master's degrees between 1951 and 1970. Slightly more than half ultimately received a doctorate degree and at least three expected to graduate in 1983—13 to 16 years after receiving the master's degree. Achievements were interesting:

    a) Of the 137 research master's students, 73% obtained their PhD. More surprising is the fact that one in three of the professional master's had a doctorate by 1982. It appeared that this did not happen simply to gain certification since a quarter who graduated prior to 1962 had their doctorate by 1965, when the necessity for this degree was becoming evident.

b) While 80% of the research master's with PhDs received this from McGill, so too did almost half of the MSc Applied graduates; an equal number graduated from American or European universities.

c) I was interested in the proportion of each group who identified with psychology through membership in psychological associations for which I had directories. There was little or no difference between the two groups: 60% of each considered themselves psychologists through membership in the CPA, APA, the Quebec Corporation, or the Ontario Board of Examiners in Psychology.

d) Occupational histories of the two groups were different in ways to be expected but there were surprises as well:

- A quarter of all graduates were professors in 1982: 43% of research graduates; 10% of professionals.

- Of all graduates, 20% were salaried clinicians or counsellors. It is not surprising that this included 35% of the professionals, but seven (6%) research master's were clinicians.

- Few were in private practice as psychologists: six professionals and five researchers. At least one of the latter was in clinical psychology, while two were management consultants. Two professionals were market research consultants, although we offered no training in this area.

- It is not surprising that 12 with research degrees held appointments as research workers; but three professionals were also employed in non-professional research.

- Most discouraging of all findings was the fact that those who followed the industrial/organizational sequence and were trained in personnel departments, had all dropped out of psychology and identified themselves with personnel, industrial relations, or other management careers.

UNIVERSITÉ DE MONTRÉAL

The material that follows is based on a book chapter by Father Noel Mailloux (1984), Granger's (1982) contribution to *History of Academic Psychology in Canada*, the 1966 CPA Archives, and a two-hour talk I had with Father Mailloux in 1985 discussing an earlier draft of this chapter. Also, of course, it reflects my personal recollections of Mailloux and his work as far back as 1940.

REVEREND FATHER NOEL MAILLOUX, OP

The Rector of the Université de Montréal travelled to Ottawa early in 1942 to invite a young Dominican priest, Father Noel Mailloux (1909–1997), to establish an Institute of Experimental Psychology in his university. Thus began the history not only of experimental psychology in French Canada, but of professional psychology. To appreciate what Mailloux accomplished requires some knowledge of the man himself.

Born in Quebec in 1909, Mailloux received his BA from the Université de Montréal in 1930 and went to Rome where, in 1934, he received his PhD with a thesis on mental health and fatigue. Three years later, he was ordained a priest in the Dominican Order and obtained his Licentiate in Sacred Theology in 1938. During his seven years in Rome, he had studied psychology intensely, particularly the German psychologists. In addition, he had become interested in psychoanalysis and the writings of Freud. A linguist, he developed a wide range of friends and acquaintances among European psychologists.

Father Mailloux returned to North America, where he joined Professor A. G. Bills of the University of Cincinnati as a post-doctoral fellow. For the next year, he continued his studies of mental work and fatigue with mentally ill hospital patients and broadened his knowledge of abnormal psychology. Any thought of returning to Rome for an academic research career in Europe ended with the outbreak of war. Mailloux returned to Canada, where he was professor of experimental psychology from 1940 to 1942 in the Faculty of Philosophy and Theology at the Dominican College in Ottawa. It was from there that the rector of the university invited him to Montreal.

During his three years in Ottawa, Mailloux became known in French Canada not only as intellectually able, but as one who could present the lay science of psychology in a manner understandable and acceptable in French-Canadian academic and clerical circles. He had brought Canadian and American professors to several symposia in Ottawa and had edited and published four books that were well received. The theme of mental health and education ran through all four volumes as well as a number of journal articles.

One must recognize that Mailloux's background is unique among North American psychologists in order to appreciate what he brought to the Université de Montréal. He was a linguist and, as I have mentioned, knew most European psychologists. On his return to North America, he quickly expanded his acquaintanceships to include many North American leaders. An avid reader, he sought communication with his peers whatever their language or religion.

Father Mailloux was 32 when he organized the Institut de Psychologie (Psychological Institute). He was an unhyphenated psychologist in the sense that typified most pre-1930s trained academics. He could not fairly be called an experimentalist or a professional or an applied or social psychologist, although he had interests in these and other areas. He was a psychologist with a dream to bring together a group of professors and students united in the search for an understanding of what makes man a man. Such knowledge would be sought for use in service to man. Fulfillment of this dream required speculation, research including field study, collaboration with students in other disciplines, and, of course, an effort to make useful application that would involve professional activities. In short, the dream required academic researchers and professionals to understand each other and work together for the maximum achievement of each.

Mailloux never faltered in his effort to fulfil this dream. Consequently, the separation of professional from academic training, particularly in the early years, is not always clear. Mailloux, in fact, came up with a "scientist-professional" model that trained clinicians well before a similar terminology was adopted by American academics at the 1950 Boulder Conference.

INSTITUT DE PSYCHOLOGIE

THE EARLY YEARS

By September 1942, Mailloux had, on paper, a three-year programme of study leading to three degrees; he had engaged ten part-time lecturers, some of whom were professors in the faculties of medicine and science. Finally, he had an enrollment of seven students. This was the beginning.

The actual directions along which the Institut de Psychologie developed were shaped largely by events of which Mailloux took advantage. After all, he had a very limited budget, little space, only part-time staff, and very few students.

The first "break" came in 1943 when the Catholic Charities of Montreal asked him to establish a residential centre (Centre d'Orientation) to provide treatment to gifted children handicapped by emotional problems. This provided a field setting where ideas could be turned into action, research coordinated with this, and students could receive training as preparation for professional work. Mailloux personally gave liberally of his time to this centre for more than 30 years. Basically, the treatment orientation from the beginning was psychoanalytical.

The establishment of a Montreal group to study problems of psychoanalysis was a natural outgrowth of this treatment centre. With two psychoanalytically oriented psychiatrists, Karl Stern and Migel Prados, he brought together a group that for years met regularly and was the forerunner of the Canadian Association for Psychoanalysis.

As might be expected, psychoanalytic theory quickly (1943) became included in the curriculum: first as part of a course in abnormal psychology, and then, in 1949, such teaching became an official part of the programme. Dr. Gabrielle Clerk (née Brunet, 1923–2012) has given a brief description of professional training in the early days (Clerk, 1984). The core curriculum included many courses in psychoanalytical clinical psychology, including psychopathology and projective tests. There was also a strong emphasis on research, although she suggests that Anglo-Saxon colleagues would probably view the programme as more closely related to the humanities than to science. She also noted that the Institut de Psychologie staff was supplemented by many visiting professors both from Europe and from North America.

Another event occurred, this time in 1944, that Mailloux was able to turn to good advantage in the training of professionals. One of his students, Julien Beausoleil, commenced work on a thesis topic related to delinquency and criminality. Not only did this interest people in several academic circles, but it led the provincial government to seek the institut's assistance in a major project for the re-education of young delinquents. Mailloux did not publish his first paper on this subject until 1959, but over the years the institut's work in this area created world-wide attention. For our purposes, it is sufficient to note that this was another field situation that not only opened significant research but enabled the institut to produce another kind of professional.

Other events in the early days enabled the institut to develop in directions more closely related to the academic than to the professional side. Mailloux became closely involved with the psychology of religion and its relation to mental health while some of his students, particularly Adrien Pinard, who had been one of the original seven in 1942, and Dr. Thérèse Décarie turned to the study of intelligence in young children. Pinard noticed that American psychologists had misinterpreted much of Piaget's thrust, and so when Piaget attended the International Congress of Psychology in Montreal (1954), it was the group at the Institut that welcomed him and later established his reputation in North America. This event almost certainly influenced some of the professionals who later entered private practice or became school psychologists.

Clinical training dominated even in the early years, but training was broader. Students were sent to American universities to prepare to train industrial psychologists, but my impression is that they felt more comfortable dealing with persons in university business schools than with those in the two mainstreams of psychology: the clinical and the academic.

MORE RECENT DEVELOPMENTS

The original three-year programme of study was modified. As early as 1946, two years were required for the doctorate, and in 1953, it was agreed to withhold the professional doctorate until one year of professional practice had been completed. Complications soon appeared. Professional students had been relatively inactive in the Psychological Association of the Province of Quebec and, after completing the academic programme, became professionals. The official response of the Institut de Psychologie was to shift one year of study from the doctorate to the master's level. It should be noted that once the corporation had replaced the Quebec society, this same group stopped a move to require the doctorate for corporation membership.

The institut expanded over the years. Mailloux was granted two associate professors in 1948. The full-time staff had increased to 14 by 1954, to 16 by 1960, and to 42 by 1969. Basic academic research developed during these years, particularly in the study of intellectual development and physiological psychology.

Mailloux resigned as director in 1957 and was replaced by Dr. Adrien Pinard. That year the curriculum was changed to offer ten areas of specialization at the doctoral level. Five appear to have been in professional fields: clinical, psychometrics, and projective techniques; industrial and vocational guidance; delinquency and criminology; and military psychology. A year later, Pinard reduced the ten areas to five.

Pinard (1964) was not happy with the product of a scientist-professional model of clinical training at his or at other North American universities. He used the occasion of his CPA presidential address in 1964 to draw attention to the low scientific publication rate among graduates of such programmes and announced that his university would offer two complementary but different programmes: one to produce professionals; the other academic researchers. Dr. David Belanger had introduced these changes when he succeeded Pinard as director in 1963.

The courses of study were modified: The BA required two years (later this was increased to three), the master's was reduced to one year, and the doctorate required two years. Those in the professional stream received the Master of Psychology degree while doctorate candidates worked for the Doctor in Psychology. The academic research programme continued to offer the MA and PhD. This division led to much conflict, and in 1969 (this takes us beyond the official close of this history and these reflections), staff voted to create two separate entities, each responsible for its own programme. This decision was never implemented, as Mailloux was requested to return as chairman, and his vision of the department continued to require unity in one organization designed to produce both professionals and experimental academics. This, it should be noted, did not end the conflict, and a group of academics successfully petitioned in 1975 to create an autonomous Department of Academic Psychology. The department was divided, and as recently as 1982, Granger (1982) reported conflict continued to manifest itself.

THE GRADUATES

Figures are not available as to the number of professional and academic graduates, their degrees, or occupational distribution. Some information about some graduates is available from the 1966 CPA Directory. One hundred Institut de Psychologie graduates were either members or associates of the CPA, and they represented 10% of membership. The directory provides information that helps clarify our knowledge of those who belonged to the CPA. I present this with serious reservations, as these individuals cannot possibly be a cross section of institut graduates. The very nature of the CPA structure in earlier years must have discouraged those not fluent in English. It was not practical for a member to speak or write in French within the association.

This generalization requires justification. During the CPA's first 27 years (1940–1966), only three presidents and seven of the 49 directors had French as their mother-tongue. It is true that from 1959 to 1966, one French-Canadian was on the board every year, but there was no one in six of the preceding 13 years. The position of secretary treasurer was filled by 13 psychologists between 1940 and 1966; not one could carry on correspondence or a conversation in French. There was no paid secretarial staff to offer this service.

An attempt was made to have Quebec professionals represented by the Psychological Association of the Province of Quebec, which Mailloux and Frances Alexander (from McGill) had founded during the war years. The principal language was English; institut graduates, as has been noted, had their own organization until the corporation was established; they promptly took it over.

The 100 CPA members and associates received 162 degrees from the institut. The largest number (91) received the master's, but 43 obtained their BA and 28 the doctorate. While these figures are unlikely to represent all students, one finding may be more or less typical of graduates. Almost half received two degrees from the university, while 11 received three. Most others received only the master's, although two CPA members left on receiving their BA and took higher degrees at another university. The CPA membership reflects growth of graduates—at least to some degree. Only four of those who graduated during the years 1943 to 1946 were members in 1966; 20 from the next five years are in the directory as are some 25 from each of the three following five-year periods.

Mailloux's early objective appears to have been to graduate about equal numbers of academic researchers and professionals. Almost certainly he failed in this, as professionals predominated even within CPA membership. The sample must be reduced from 100 to 85, as 15 members did not list their occupations. Most of these were married women, who were probably out of the workforce at least temporarily. Only 24 of the 85 reported academic positions in universities or colleges. On the other hand, 51 were professionals, which included 30 in clinical positions with the remainder employed in industry, schools, or guidance and counselling centres. Ten were out of psychology or in administrative positions that were marginal.

By the time of Couchiching and the end of this historical period, the Institut de Psychologie was a professional source to be reckoned with.

CHAPTER 6

EARLY PROFESSIONAL
PSYCHOLOGISTS AND THE CPA:

THE INTERPLAY

NO PERSON, GROUP, OR ORGANIZATION, EXCEPT for the British and federal governments (through the British North America Act), has influenced the growth of the profession as has the Canadian Psychological Association (CPA). This chapter summarizes the history of the CPA until the Couchiching Conference, focussing on the impact of the CPA on the profession and the reasons for this.

This chapter is considerably different from what I had anticipated. Let me start by explaining how and why.

Within weeks of his election to association president in 1949, J. S. A. Bois phoned me to say he had just read the minutes of early meetings of the CPA Executive (the minutes have disappeared) and discovered that the executive had questioned whether he and I should be admitted to membership. Both of us had reported principal allegiance to private practice. We were consultants—that is, professionals (a word not introduced until after World War II). For more than 30 years, I firmly believed the CPA to be anti-professional. Indeed, I was not alone in this view, as I alluded to earlier in Chapter 3. However, after studying the CPA Archives while preparing this book, I became convinced that, without the CPA from 1939 to some point in the 1950s, psychology would never have developed as a reasonably acceptable profession. At best, it might have ranked with chiropractic and chiropody.

I feel required to justify my conversion and my inclination to forgive a number of actions clearly designed to thwart a viable profession. These actions, I am now convinced, reflected misconceptions and fears of well-intentioned men, frightened and disturbed about what they had created—yet they did not give up. They continued to work for a Canadian association with which they could live—something many professionals did not do.

While I hope the history is reported objectively, the interpretation of some of the events and actions is through the eyes of and mind of an avowed professional. The chapter is organized into two sections: Pre-1945 and Post-1945, roughly paralleling the war years.

WAR-TIME FOUNDATIONS

The American Psychological Association (APA) was founded to represent the interests of Canada as well as the United States, and generally it served this purpose well. Objectives and activities were, of course, determined by the needs of American members. Wright (1974) estimated there were about 50 psychologists in Canada as late as 1938. While this probably is an underestimate, the number was almost certainly less than 100.

Some of the senior Canadian psychologists began to question the wisdom of our reliance on APA in view of world affairs. Chamberlain capitulated to Hitler in 1938, and before the end of the year, war between Great Britain and Germany appeared inevitable. Canada, as part of the Empire, would be involved from the beginning. Almost certainly the United States would not be, and American-controlled organizations would be strictly neutral.

Apparently in the latter part of 1938, there was personal correspondence among some professors of psychology that raised the issue of a Canadian association designed to spearhead approaches to the government that would assure psychologists would have an opportunity to contribute to the war effort. When, in December 1938, the American Association for the Advancement of Science (AAAS) met in Ottawa, the few Canadians present got together informally to discuss what could be done to prepare for the outbreak of war. This, while strictly informal, was the first important meeting that would lead ultimately to the formation of the CPA. It was agreed a formal association would be required. Professor J. M. MacEachern (1877–1971), chairman of the Department of Philosophy and Psychology, University of Alberta, agreed to prepare a draft constitution while Professor David Ketchum (University of Toronto) and Professor N. W. Morton (McGill University) undertook a survey of Canadian resources for psychological research. It was agreed to hold a meeting of Canadian psychologists in the spring of 1939.

It seems to me most unlikely that psychology's contributions to the war effort nor the foundation upon which post-war professionalism developed would have occurred without a national association to deal with the government. My evidence to support this perspective can be found in our efforts in Montreal through the Psychological Institute and Opinion Surveys Limited in the weeks immediately before and after the declaration of war. As discussed in Chapter 4, we made a two-pronged approach to Ottawa:

- Basing recommendations on our work selecting and placing applicants under the Youth Training Plan, we attempted to interest the minister of National Defence with our potential role in personnel selection in the military. We did not have the opportunity to see him personally, as his reply to our submission consisted simply of four lines that stated his officers were quite competent to select and assign recruits without outside help.

- At the same time, basing a proposal on the achievements of Opinion Surveys Limited, we, together with a group of public relations specialists, made representation to Cabinet regarding public opinion, psychological warfare, and public information. This was presented to Cabinet but was considered unnecessary.

On April 12, 1939, a meeting was held in Toronto as a follow-up to the one in December 1938. There does not appear to be a record of who attended, but it was agreed among those there that a national association was required and that its primary task was to get Canadian psychology involved in the conduct of the war that appeared imminent. Canadian Psychological Association was accepted as the name of the organization. Three officers were elected: Professor E. A.

Bott, University of Toronto, who was president; Professor George Humphrey (1889–1966), Queen's University, who was secretary; and Professor Ray B. Liddy (1886–1961), University of Western Ontario, who was treasurer. Thus, the chairmen of the psychology departments in three Ontario universities were the original officers.

This April 1939 meeting was important to the direction of professional psychology. Apart from the fact it produced an association that could deal with government, it set up a test development committee whose contribution undoubtedly coloured professional work for at least five or ten years after World War II.

These officers of the CPA influenced professionalism. E. A. Bott had contributed to the Canadian effort in World War I through founding, expanding, and directing a rehabilitation centre for war-impaired soldiers. This work was recognized in that he was appointed honorary captain in the Royal Canadian Medical Corps. Throughout the 1920s and 1930s, he had strong leanings towards "applied psychology," particularly in the field of mental health, as an activity of an academic psychologist. I doubt if Bott ever whole-heartedly approved of a profession independent of universities or government (as did his opposite number at McGill, W. D. Tait). A reading of Wright and Myers (1982) suggests that neither Humphrey nor Liddy had any particular interest in the applied field, let alone the professional.

Thus, the new association was in the hands of three men—one with major applied interests who had contributed in World War I, but the other two had no such background interests. It was only when Sam Bois and I applied for membership and represented ourselves as independent professionals that the existence of such people had to be recognized. Between 1939 and 1945, all three CPA officers learned much.

Membership qualification, as recommended by Professor MacEachern in the preparation of a constitution, reflected the world in which he and his associates lived. The only psychologists they recognized were those at universities, normal schools, and government. Had C. R. Myers of Toronto or N. W. Morton of McGill headed a local committee to define membership qualifications, there almost certainly would have been major differences. Presumably Myers, who was devoting half of his work to the Ontario Department of Health, would have included clinicians—at least those employed by government—while Morton would have included independent clinicians and industrial psychologists. (There were no Quebec psychologists employed by the provincial government.)

Two classes of membership were established at this meeting: members and associates (Constitution of the CPA 1940. Unpublished. Archives of the Canadian Psychological Association).

- *Member*: "A doctorate based in part on psychological study. Primarily engaged in academic, professional or administrative work in psychology; or any other person may be recommended for membership by the Council for sufficient reason, which must be stated at the time nomination is made."

- *Associate*: "A person with Honours Bachelor's degree in psychology who is continuing in graduate work in psychology, or a similar field, will be eligible one year after graduation. Those with a graduate degree are immediately eligible; others with professional qualifications may be recommended by members for their known psychological interests."

Members would pay a $2 annual fee; and associates $1.

It is important that professionals note the problems faced by MacEachern and his associates in defining membership requirements. They saw members as academics and provincial government officials who held doctorates, together with psychiatrists, and normal school instructors holding a PhD or EdD degree. They saw associates as graduate students in psychology or education; school superintendents with a graduate degree in psychology or education; and professional social workers, physiologists, biologists and others with interest in psychology.

The most important single action taken at the April 1939 meeting was to establish a committee, chaired by Professor Liddy, to develop a selection test for use in the armed services. The constitution drafted by MacEachern was considered, but it was agreed it would not come into effect until the end of the war—except for the conditions of membership.

Liddy's committee sought and ultimately received money from the president of the National Research Council to pay for the development of a test for military use, while Morton organized a group to develop a test that could be printed when money became available. Others, particularly Bott, developed contacts with government, and as reported in Chapter 4, Canadian psychologists proceeded to apply their know-how and "guess-how" to military problems.

The efforts of all Canadian psychologists from 1939 until 1945 were divided between either contributing directly to the war effort or carrying very heavy civilian loads, which included the duties of others directly involved with the war. This work is discussed further in Chapter 4.

Wright (1974) listed the 53 people she knew of who were psychologists working in Canada in 1938. This list is seriously incomplete. All but two are listed in the 1946 CPA Directory. In 1938, several she listed were still students, but by 1946, 43 had a doctorate (PhD or DPaed); the remaining had MA degrees. None appears to have been in government service or to have been in normal schools in the West—yet MacEachern appears to have had both these categories in mind when he recommended membership qualifications. McGill, in 1938, recognized several psychologists working in Montreal, some with the MA and at least one with no degree. Probably there were others with the BA. Even as early as the spring of 1946, Professor William Line of the University of Toronto verbally recommended to the Department of Veterans' Affairs group meeting in Montreal that the Honours BA should be accepted as the basic degree for a clinical psychologist. Wright does not include any BAs.

Whatever the actual deliberations of psychologists in the Association in 1938 or 1940, the picture changed substantially over the years. The change in make-up of membership in the CPA during the war years is the one non-military thing of importance to the profession. While interest up to this point is the pre-1945 period, the following tables, based on my analysis of the CPA directories for the respective years, summarize the situation in 1938 and 1945, and anticipate the trajectory of the association during the subsequent 20 years.

Table 1 includes the number of CPA members from 1938 to 1967. In 1938, there were 52 members, increased to 238 in 1945 and then to 952 in 1967, at the time of the Couchiching Conference. It also shows the highest degree held by those members.

TABLE 1

	1938	1945	1956	1967
Number of members	52	238	607	952
Doctorate	35 (57%)	76 (33%)	173 (28%)	492 (52%)
Master's	14 (27%)	84 (35%)	228 (38%)	432 (45%)
Bachelor's	1 (2%)	51 (21%)	47 (8%)	23 (2%)
MD	0	5 (2%)	5(1%)	1 (0.1%)
Total known degree status	50	216	453	948
Not known or reported	2 (4%)	22 (9%)	154 (25%)	4 (1%)

Table 2 shows the areas of reported occupation of Canadian psychologists listed in CPA directories for 1945, 1956, and 1967.

TABLE 2

	1945	1956	1967
Number of members	221	624	967
Employment settings:			
Academic and research	29%	27%	42%
Clinical	3%	16%	18%
Guidance and counselling	7%	6%	7%
School/education	1%	2%	4%
Industrial	0%	7%	3%
Military and Defence Research Board	29%	5%	2%

Continued...

. . . *continued*

	1945	1956	1967
Government	6%	6%	3%
Consulting and private practice	2%	2%	3%
Non-psychological	12%	9%	5%
Not reported	12%	21%	13%
Number of student members	17	122	236
Retired members	0	0	5
Total members	**238**	**746**	**1208**

We see in this table an increase in the percentage of members employed in academic and research settings and employed as clinical psychologists and, not surprisingly, a decrease in those employed in military settings and the Defence Research Board and those employed in non-psychology settings.

The first general meeting of the CPA was held at McGill University in 1940. At least 50 attended the presented papers, and Wright (1974) reported that the 26 who attended the business meeting were the charter members. At the business meeting, it was agreed that the constitution would come into effect at the end of the war, but the original terms of membership were to be as included in the Annual Meeting Minutes: "Applications may be made by those who hold a graduate degree based in part on psychological study or who are actively interested in the advancement of psychology as a science or profession." Annual meetings were held in 1942 and 1944 in Toronto, while the 1945 meeting was in Montreal. Paid membership in 1942 was 80; in 1944, 123 plus 34 not paid; and 158 in 1945.

The 1945 meeting is particularly important in the history of professional psychology. Not only was the constitution basically approved (although amended in May 1947 and published in the *Canadian Journal of Psychology*, 1947, vol. 1(3), p. 157–159), but the association adopted By-Law 1:

"The Council of the Association organize a Board of Certification. The Board shall be empowered to:

1. Establish qualification of applicants for certification;
2. Examine qualification of applicants for certification;
3. Issue and cancel certificates of certification as a Psychologist;
4. Elect a Registrar who shall keep the records of certification;
5. Charge a fee for such certification."

So began the role of the Canadian Psychological Association in the post-war development of professional psychology in Canada.

THE IMMEDIATE POST-WAR YEARS

[*Editors' note: The pre-1945 material for this chapter was written entirely by ECW; much of the post-1945 material was found in piecemeal draft form and rough handwritten notes by ECW and required reworking by WGW and DEGW. We, of course, do not bring the same perspective, experiences, engagement, and insight as ECW would have, and accordingly, the post-1945 section should be read and interpreted with this in mind.*]

As is evident in tables 1 and 2 included in the previous section, the 20-year period from the end of World War II in 1945 until the convening of the Couchiching Conference in May, 1966 saw notable growth in the Canadian Psychological Association and notable changes in the composition of the membership. Table 3 shows the growth in numbers and the membership status of CPA members over the years:

TABLE 3

	1949	1952	1953	1954	1957
Fellows and members	154	181	190	216	250
Associates	257	359	310	381	361
Student affiliates	109	98	79	109	150
Hon. life fellows	1				6
Hon. life member	2				
Total	**523**	**638**	**579**	**706**	**767**

	1958	1959	1960	1966
Fellows and members	239	238	194	294
Associates	346	364	237	593
Student affiliates	138	137	85	213
Hon. life fellows	6	6	?	7
Hon. life member				12
Total	**729**	**745**	**708**	**1119**

[*Editors' note: A review of ECW's notes from the CPA Archives suggests that while the total membership for 1960 is probably correct, the membership category numbers for that year must, for some reason, be incorrect.*]

In preparation for the Couchiching Conference that will be discussed at the end of this chapter, a survey was conducted during the winter months of 1964 to 1965 by D. Sydiaha at the request of the Professional Affairs Committee of the CPA. The results (Sydiaha, 1966) indicated the following demographic information about members, fellows, and student affiliates:

Membership status: 271 members; 593 associates; 23 fellows; 19 honorary fellows and members; 213 students. [*Editors' note: For comparison, there are currently (2023) more than 7,000 CPA members.*]

Gender: 792 male and 323 female respondents;

Language: 925 Anglophone; 194 Francophone;

Highest degree: 490 MA degree; 431 PhD; 170 BA; 29 no degree indicated;

Professional identification: 428 academic; 48 government; 428 professional.

Another snapshot of Canadian psychology in 1966 was provided by M. H. Appley and J. Richwood (1967). In their survey, which examined levels of education and principal work function, an attempt was made to reach all psychologists in Canada; 1827 non-students were approached; 1234 replies were received. The results of the survey are summarized in Table 4.

TABLE 4

Principal Work Function	Sample No.	%	% with PhD	% with master's only	% with bachelor's only
Administration	161	16.3	39.1	28.6	32.3
Clinical	79	8.0	29.1	38.0	32.3
Counselling	57	5.8	14.0	52.6	33.4
Compu/stats	7	0.7	14.3	57.1	28.6
Research	118	11.9	60.2	14.4	25.4
Teach psychol	169	17.1	71.0	11.2	17.8
Teach other	29	2.9	31.0	24.1	44.9
Writing	8	0.8	50.0	25.0	25.0
Testing	152	15.3	11.2	49.3	39.5
Personnel	29	2.9	34.5	34.5	31.0
Other	21	2.1	9.5	14.3	76.2
No response	160	16.2	26.9	34.9	36.2
Total	**990**	**100**	**37.3**	**30.8**	**31.9**

Inclusion of the four CPA membership tables is intended simply to convey something of the changing nature of the CPA over the post-war years, culminating in the mid-1960s—the end point of the period of these reflections. The growth in membership numbers is certainly evident, but equally important is the changing distribution of work functions of the members.

CERTIFICATION

Despite the CPA having been comprised largely of academics, and despite the presidency having been held by academics in all but three years, the CPA has from the start been concerned with issues affecting the development and practice of professional psychology.

As noted earlier in this chapter, the CPA adopted in 1945 one by-law that instructed Council to organize a board of certification.

Part of the context of the time was *The Weir Report on Rehabilitation* (1943) that stated that 150 psychologists were needed in Ontario and 450 in Canada. It did not detail what they were needed for, but the post-war professional training situation was described:

> The situation is rendered critical in our universities by the multitude of students (ex-service as well as non-service) and the dearth of qualified staff. During the war years our national services had with them sufficient psychologists with teaching experience to do their own training for psychological specialties but now these services are leaning heavily on our universities to conduct special training for them. This interim condition should presently give place to a sound form of regular training in psychology which would more nearly meet the practical needs of our country.

E. A. Bott was asked for an opinion on By-Law 1 that had been approved in 1945. In his report (Bott, 1947), he emphasized that under Article II of the constitution, the objective of the CPA is "to promote the advancement *and* [italics are his] practical application of psychological studies in Canada." Three means are mentioned: teaching, discussion, and research. The justification for certification is found in the three recognized activities of the CPA, that includes "any other activities calculated to further the association's objectives" (Bott,

1947, p. 4). He went on to comment that the first move by the association to authorize means beyond "teaching, discussion, and research" was taken in the previous year with the approval of By-Law 1 and the specification of the powers of a board of certification.

Bott (1947) proceeded in his report to list the different components that may be required for various kinds of professional work, and he considered how much of a public need exists for certification. How broad a field would certification cover?

Certification might be controlled in the public sector. Private employment would be hard to control, but self-employment would be most difficult because one person is responsible for two functions: professional service and profit-making. He concluded: "Generally speaking a certification scheme should make a greater contribution to a community if framed to meet the positive needs of public service rather than if designed primarily to curb possible abuses that may occasionally arise under self-employment" (Bott, 1947, p. 7).

Finally, and prescient of things to come, he doubted if a training organization, scientific body, or professional association could in fact establish certification. This would require a legally constituted public body that stands between a special group and the public to be serviced. "In short, certification must be by some proper governmental authority, either provincial or federal or both" (p. 7). Interestingly enough, no one, including Bott himself, seemed to fully appreciate at the time the significance and implications of what he was suggesting.

Bott (1947) concluded that the body that the CPA was to establish under By-Law 1 should function as a standing committee rather than as a board of certification, and that it should concentrate its efforts on establishing certification. It should also work on a code of ethics.

E. S. W. Belyea delivered a paper, "Psychology as a Profession in Canada," to the second Annual Conference of the BC Academy of Sciences and Affiliated Societies (April 6, 1948). He reported on what happened following Bott's report. A study committee on certification was established at the 1946 annual meeting, with Bois as chairman. It presented a rather long report to the 1947 annual meeting. There was, however, little discussion, the report was adopted, and a new standing committee was established, with Belyea as chairman. At the

1948 annual meeting (Myers, 1948), prompted by the 1947 committee report, there was much interest in the issue of certification, and the annual meeting approved a motion that, "the Executive of the Association shall organize, between now and the next Annual Meeting, a Canadian Board of Examiners in Professional Psychology . . . [that would be] independent in its finances and activities from the [Canadian Psychological] Association." This followed a strong exhortation from the Psychological Association of the Province of Quebec that such a board of examiners be established.

Interestingly, Bois, writing from his perspective as chair of the CPA Committee on Certification and chair of a parallel committee of the Psychological Association of the Province of Quebec, had separately advocated establishment of a national board. "Let us create a Board of Professional Examiners sponsored by and recognized by our Associations but independent of them in its finances and its activities. If there are enough practicing psychologists in Canada who realize that certification is an urgent problem that concerns them more than anyone else, let these pool their resources and finance the setting up of such a Board" (Bois, 1948, p. 10).

Belyea (1948) pointed out that "while such a solution may be obvious in its structure, its achievement is blocked by many obstacles. Not the least of these is the very small number of persons who would be certifiable on any reasonable basis and who are actually practicing in Canada today. The bulk of psychologists are in types of employment which are not directly affected and, as a consequence, such persons are inclined to advocate a policy of cautious advance on the problem."

Belyea's committee had a number of recommendations, including:

1. recognition that all fellows and members of the CPA have a certain degree of professional competence;

2. membership requirements to be modified to ensure (1); and

3. the CPA to set up comprehensive professional examinations to be taken by all who received the MA.

Apparently, I was a member of the committee but recall nothing about it. The report was prepared by three BC members who had met once.

Meanwhile, employers were establishing expectations for employment of psychologists. For example, the CPA Archives contain a note (Nov. 1, 1946) "for the file" from C. R. Myers, psychologist, Department of Health, stating that the BC provincial government classification of jobs provides or defines:

- Clinical assistant: BA with major in psychology and associate membership in the CPA.

- Psychologist: MA in psychology and several years experience; full membership in the CPA.

At the time (1946), there were two psychologists and two clinical assistants.

COMMITTEE ON PROFESSIONAL STANDARDS

In 1949, the Committee on Professional Standards had made arrangements with American Board of Examiners in Professional Psychology (ABEPP) for members or fellows of the CPA to apply for the ABEPP Diploma either through the grandfather clause or by examination. Members were notified of this agreement in the fall of 1949. In November 1950, the Executive authorized $100 for the committee to meet and gave it powers to act. It was to deal with ABEPP on the certification of Canadian psychologists by ABEPP. The chief problem was seen to be the establishment of a mutually satisfying set of principles that would define the committee's scope and its relationship with ABEPP. Specific problems foreseen were grandfather clause applicants, French language examinations, and intermediate certificate.

In the subsequent year or two, the committee reviewed applications by 33 persons referred by ABEPP. The committee would not recommend or endorse candidates (despite the committee's terms of reference) but would comment on the adequacy of proposed endorsers and indicate the applicant's status in the CPA. At its meeting on February 13, 1952, the executive "reaffirmed at the request of Bois to liaise with ABEPP, attempt to keep provincial standards for certification comparable, and continually review provincial certification needs and be prepared to advise."

Following from its terms of reference, the committee also at this time considered issuing certificates at the intermediate level and examined the authority of the CPA to undertake such certification. It concluded its legal capabilities were limited to definition on objective grounds for distinct classes of membership. Therefore, it proposed for consideration by members a class of "senior psychologist," qualifications for which would be:

- two years full membership in the CPA;

- a PhD or equivalent or demonstrated competency in the practice of psychology for five years; and

- evidence of professional integrity.

The Committee on Professional Standards did not meet in 1952, but it did review again intermediate certification and senior membership. Committee members were negative to the senior membership category, and on February 13, 1952, the executive advised the committee to drop the senior membership issue. The committee recommended a certification board be set up in each province. It also submitted to the various provincial associations the standards for an intermediate certification that it had established.

At about this time, roughly 10 years after Bott had expressed his concern about the legal status of national professional certification, a letter was received from the Department of the Secretary of State and discussed by the Official Board of Council on June 1, 1955. "This Department cannot purport to authorize an organization to set an examination as a condition for membership and to issue documentary evidence of such qualification. It will be appreciated that such matters of issue of degrees and the like fall into the exclusive jurisdiction of the Provinces." The directors concluded that provincial associations should handle certification.

At this same time (1955), Dr. O. K. Ault had become chairman of the Committee on Professional Standards and was asked by the executive to continue his current programme of collecting data on the various aspects of professional psychology and, in addition, to set up a sub-committee. The sub-committee would advise the CPA through the committee on what the association should do to further the prospects of professional psychologists in all provinces.

In April 1956, Ault presented the sub-committee's report that clearly indicated it had become thoroughly familiar with issues around certification. The sub-committee recognized that protection of the public is the jurisdiction of provinces, not national organizations. He questioned how the CPA could help in general and how in particular it could help provincial organizations. The decision was made to keep in close touch with provincial organizations, and possible directions for the future were raised: Higher standards for membership? Revised by-laws? Or a committee to advise on and coordinate the progressive efforts of the provincial organizations towards certification?

PSYCHOLOGY ACROSS CANADA—PROVINCIAL ASSOCIATIONS

In 1958, the Committee on Professional Standards focussed on staying in close touch with various professional organizations across Canada interested in promoting the professional status of psychologists, and reported (Wake, 1958) the highlights of its study of progress in the provinces. It noted the following:

- No activity in the Atlantic provinces.

- In Quebec, the Corporation of Psychologists of the Province of Quebec was created through Letters Patent on August 28, 1956, and first meeting was held September 1956. It established two classes of membership:

    - Psychologist: requiring a post-graduate degree in psychology from a recognized university or its equivalent.

    - Consultant psychologist: doctoral degree plus three years of substantive professional experience; or the MA degree plus seven years.

- The Ontario Psychological Association had a draft bill but had not been able to obtain full-fledged support. Its committee on legislation was directed to survey the members with respect to attitudes towards certification and the draft bill.

- Manitoba had formed a psychology association. There were 17 members at the first meeting in September 1957. Nothing had been done about certification.

- Saskatchewan Psychological Association had prepared a draft bill, fashioned after the proposed Ontario Act. It was optimistic that the bill would be passed by the legislature in 1959.

- In Alberta, no progress was reported in forming a psychology association.

- The British Columbia Psychological Association had adopted a constitution and by-law that involved a new classification of members.

In 1962, the CPA received further correspondence from the Secretary of State, which stated: "CPA can set any standards it wants for its members and reject those it believes unsuitable. It has no control over persons who are not members. Only a province can establish bodies to provide control."

On May 30, 1962, possibly in reaction to the second letter from the Office of the Secretary of State, the CPA Board reviewed a report of a committee on professional problems established in 1959 because of the CPA's lack of information about psychology across Canada. The board decided that the committee should be reactivated to draw up specific proposals regarding a study or studies of psychology in Canada that could be referred immediately to granting agencies for funding support. The committee contacted provincial associations and heard back from five. None was apparently working towards licencing at that time.

Certification was certainly not the only professionally related issue with which the CPA was confronted. For example, despite efforts through committees and support from the executive in 1952 and again in 1956, little progress was made with respect to professional interrelationships with the Canadian Psychiatric Association and the question of therapy. At the 1958 annual meeting, these efforts were broadened to include relationships with other allied disciplines. In another realm, R. W. Payne, associate professor and chairman of Graduate Studies, Department of Psychology, Queen's University, wrote the CPA secretary-treasurer on July 13, 1962, strongly urging the CPA to establish a set of fees for psychological services done in private practice. Because of a lack of such a fee schedule, psychologists apparently could not be paid from health insurance plans. This letter was discussed by the Executive Committee, which decided that this was a matter for regional associations.

PROFESSIONAL TRAINING AT CANADIAN UNIVERSITIES

Chapter 5 reviewed the development of professional training programmes at McGill University and Université de Montréal, but professional psychology was slowly developing in universities elsewhere across Canada and much of it had a clinical focus. Much of this history is discussed at length in Wright and Myers (1982). In light of these developments, the Committee on Clinical Training had been appointed by the CPA Board in 1956 and developed recommendations "dealing with what it considered to be some of the essential ingredients or aspects of a model clinical training program" (Wright, 1957). These boiled down to the following:

- A broad undergraduate education provides a strong foundation.

- Research skills are the most valuable asset of our profession.

- Training in diagnostic testing is essential.

- Training should include an opportunity to know patients first hand and share responsibility for some phases of their psychological care.

- Supervised internship is indispensable.

- A doctoral degree is necessary.

At this time, members of the committee resigned, apparently and provocatively "because of new professional duties," and a search was undertaken to appoint a new chair. Following the MacLeod Report in 1955 (discussed in Chapter 1), Dr. E. Poser, who agreed with MacLeod's unhappiness with teaching techniques and other applied courses for undergraduates, was offered the chairmanship of the Committee on Clinical Training. He turned it down in a letter (December 7, 1957) to Dr. R. Bromiley. His problem was that the executive paid no attention to what he (Poser) thought were some highly realistic recommendations:

- A board should be established to assess training programmes for all applied psychology.

- The CPA should explore the possibility of encouraging and/or sponsoring post-graduate training programmes.

Poser finally accepted chairmanship and reported to the annual business meeting June 13, 1958. According to the report of the annual meeting of the CPA in 1958, the Committee on Clinical Training recommended that the curricular requirements of the committee be reassessed. Furthermore, it recommended that the committee be disbanded because its frame of reference was being subsumed as part of a larger issue confronting the development of applied psychology.

An article by Myers (1958) had apparently changed the point of view of the directors, and the new and larger issue was reflected in the approval of a resolution at the June 1958 annual meeting that "the future of psychology in Canada at the undergraduate training levels, and in its professional and scientific development is the definite concern of the CPA, and all steps should be taken to give aggressive leadership." The association also accepted a proposal by Myers that "a conference [be held] of leading Canadian psychologists who would concern themselves with, among other things, a review of problems in the development of professional psychology in Canada."

The need for such a conference was highlighted by Mooney (1963) in reviewing the results of a survey conducted by the Committee on Clinical Training (although it had earlier been disbanded) of the heads of departments of psychology of 36 Canadian colleges and universities asking them to comment, in a structured format, on the state of clinical psychology training across the country. Mooney began his description of the results with a quote from the University of Toronto spokesman that struck a chord: "The general situation of clinical psychology in Canada at this time is a mess" (p. 77).

And so, as discussed earlier in Chapter 1, the seeds were now planted for what would be two pivotal conferences in Canadian psychology: (1) the Opinicon Conference in 1960 with the title "Training for Research in Psychology" (Bernhardt, 1961); and, because of the limited scope of Opinicon with respect to professional psychology, (2) the subsequent Couchiching Conference on

Professional Psychology in 1965 (Webster, 1967). These two conferences set the trajectory for professional psychology for the next half century.

By August 1963, planning for what would become the Couchiching Conference was on the agenda for the Executive Committee. By June 1964, the decision was made to hold the conference in Central Canada before the 1965 annual meeting. In the June 10, 1964, Executive Committee meeting, it was decided "that the importance of the proposed conference on professional problems warranted a full measure of support from the Association, including financial support if necessary." Details of the planning of the conference were outlined by W. H. Coons (1965) on behalf of the Committee on Professional Affairs.

In the April 1965 meeting, finances were high on the agenda. Four alternatives for financing the conference were discussed: The CPA pay the entire amount; pay a fixed amount; levy a special charge on all members; and/ or send a letter to delegates requesting that each delegate seek support from his organization.

The executive recognized the importance of the CPA assuming financial responsibility for this conference, but the amount requested when all other CPA budget items were considered was not available, even by using all reserves. It was therefore decided to resort to the fourth alternative with the proviso that no delegate be made to feel responsible for their own expenses. It also approved a request from Colonel Blair that I be granted funds to prepare a final report of the conference that would go to the Canada Council. That report was to be *The Couchiching Conference on Professional Psychology* (Webster, 1967), which launched the next 60 years of development of professional psychology and professional psychologists in Canada.

[Editors' note: Readers who are interested in how the professional issues described in this chapter evolved during the 15 years after the Couchiching conference might wish to read a special issue of Canadian Psychology, 1984, 25(3), pp. 177-225. The issue is comprised of a lead article by Dr. J.B. Conway on the development and status of clinical psychology training in Canada, followed by brief commentaries by 25 different leaders in the field in the 1980's.]

CONCLUDING COMMENT BY THE EDITORS

A review of the minutes and reports of meetings of the CPA executive and association committees (particularly the Committee on Professional Standards) and of correspondence contained in the CPA Archives clearly demonstrated to Edward Webster in his later years the long-standing concern of the association with professional matters and the energy that went into struggling with and ultimately addressing professionally related issues.

Edward Webster began this chapter by writing, "For more than 30 years, I firmly believed the CPA to be anti-professional. . . . However, after studying the CPA Archives . . . I became convinced that, without the CPA from 1939 to some point in the 1950s, psychology would never have developed as a reasonably acceptable profession."

Mea culpa *received and acknowledged.*

As we commented in the Preface, Edward Webster's story was unfinished in terms of a discussion of how the professional psychologists who practised during the first 40 years of the profession and who have been highlighted in these reflections actually influenced and shaped the subsequent 60 years of the profession. That will be someone else's story for tomorrow.

REFERENCES

Appley, M. H. & Richwood, J. (1967). *Psychology in Canada*, Special Study No.3. Ottawa: Science Secretariat, Privy Council Office.

Ault, O. E. (1956). Report of the Committee on Professional Standards. *Canadian Psychologist, 5*(3), 46–50.

Belyea, E. S. W. (1948, April 6). *Psychology as a profession in Canada*. Paper presented at the second Annual Conference of the BC Academy of Sciences and Affiliated Societies.

Bernhardt, K. S. (1947). Canadian psychology—past, present and future. *Canadian Journal of Psychology, 1*(2), 49–60. https://doi.org/10.1037/h0084025

Bernhardt, K. S. (Ed.). (1961). *Training for research in psychology*. University of Toronto Press.

Blair, W. R. N. (1966). In support. *Canadian Psychologist, 7a*(3), 185–196. https://doi.org/10.1037/h0083100

Bois, J.S.A. (1945a). The field of the psychological therapist. *Bulletin of the Canadian Psychological Association, 5*(3), 69-71.

Bois, J. S. A. (1945b). The field of the psychological therapist. *Journal of Clinical Psychology, 1*(4), 304–308. https://doi.org/10.1002/1097-4679(194510)1:4<304::AID-JCLP2270010412>3.0.CO;2-5

Bois, J. S. A. (1948). The certification of psychologists in Canada. *Canadian Journal of Psychology, 2*(1), 1–10. https://doi.org/10.1037/h0084046

Bott, E. A. (1947). Problems in the certification of psychologists. *Canadian Journal of Psychology, 1*(1), 3–13. https://doi.org/10.1037/h0084017

Carver, H. S. M. (1945). *Personnel selection in the Canadian Army: A descriptive study.* Ottawa: Directorate of personnel psychology, National Defence Headquarters. National Archives. Pt. 1 Reference: R10916-36-4-E, Volume/box: 1; Pt. 2 Reference: R10916-37-6-E, Volume/box: 1. Ottawa, Canada.

Carver, H. S. M. (1975). *Compassionate landscape.* University of Toronto Press.

Catano, V. M. & Tivendell, J. (1988). Industrial/organizational psychology in Canada: An introduction. *Canadian Psychology/Psychologie canadienne, 29*(1), 1–3. https://doi.org/10.1037/h0084525

Cattell, J. M. (1904). The conceptions and methods of psychology. *Popular Science Monthly, 66,* 176–186.

Clerk, G. (1984). Clinical psychology training in Canada: Its development, current status, and the prospects for accreditation. *Canadian Psychology/Psychologie canadienne, 25*(3), 205–207. https://doi.org/10.1037/h0080986

Coons, W. H. (1965). The conference on the training of professional psychologists. *Canadian Psychologist, 6a*(1, Suppl), 155–156. https://doi.org/10.1037/h0083066

Ferguson, G. A. (1982). Psychology at McGill. In Wright, M. J. & Myers, C. R. (Eds.), *History of academic psychology in Canada* (pp. 33–67). C. J. Hogrefe.

Ferguson, G. A. (1992). Psychology in Canada 1939–1945. *Canadian Psychology/Psychologie canadienne, 33*(4), 697–705. https://doi.org/10.1037/h0078747

Fox, R. E., Barclay, A. G. & Rodgers, D. A. (1982). The foundations of professional psychology. *American Psychologist, 37*(3), 306–312. https://doi.org/10.1037/0003-066X.37.3.306

Granger, L. (1982). Psychology at Montreal. In Wright, M. J. & Myers, C. R. (Eds.), *History of academic psychology in Canada* (pp. 157–164). C. J. Hogrefe.

Hebb, D. O. (1949). The *organization of behavior*. John Wiley & Sons, Inc.

Hitsman, J. M. (1946). *The problem of selection and reallocation of personnel in the Canadian Army Overseas, 1939-1946*. Canadian Military Headquarters (CMHQ). Ottawa. https://www.canada.ca/en/department-national-defence/services/military-history/history-heritage/official-military-history-lineages/reports/military-headquarters-1940-1948/selection-reallocation-problem-personnel-canadian-army-overseas-1939-1946.html

Howard, J. W. (1943). *Outline of personnel selection activities overseas*. National Archives, Reference R10916-35-2-E, Volume/box number: 1. Ottawa, Canada.

Howard, J. W. (1946a). *Tour of U.S. psychology centres—Correspondence, itineraries, papers*. National Archives, Reference R10916-38-8-E. Volume/box number: 1. Ottawa, Canada.

Howard, J. W. (1946b) *Department of National Defence—Personnel selection, correspondence, memos & procedures*. National Archives, Reference R10916-32-7-E, Volume number: 1. Ottawa, Canada.

Howard, J. W. (1984). *Correspondence with Edward C. Webster—History of Canadian psychology*. National Archives, Reference R10-916-29-7-E, Volume 1, File number 25. Ottawa, Canada.

MacLeod, R.B. (1955). *Psychology in Canadian universities and colleges*. Canadian Social Science Research Council.

Mailloux, N. (1984). L'Institut de psychologie: un groupe de professeurs et d'étudiants qui cherchent à comprendre ce qui fait que l'homme est home et peut le devenir toujours davantage. In Rocher, G. (Ed), *Continuité et rupture: Les sciences sociales au Québec, vol. 1* (pp. 27–44). Montréal: Les Presses de l'Université de Montréal.

Merriam-Webster, Incorporated. (1971). Professional. In *Webster's seventh new collegiate dictionary* (7th ed.). G&C Merriam Company.

Mooney, C. M. (1963). Clinical psychology training in Canada. *Canadian Psychologist, 4a*(3), 74–86. https://doi.org/10.1037/h0083050

Myers, C. R. (1948). Proceedings of the seventh annual meeting of the Canadian Psychological Association. *Canadian Journal of Psychology, 2*(3), 145–152.

Myers, C. R. (1958). Professional psychology in Canada. *Canadian Psychologist, 7*(2), 27–36.

Myers, C. R. (1965). Notes on the history of psychology in Canada. *Canadian Psychologist, 6a*, 4–19.

Myers, C. R. (1975–1980). *Oral history of psychology in Canada*. Canadian Psychological Association Archives.

Sydiaha, D. (1966). A survey of psychologists in Canada. *Canadian Psychologist, 7a*(5), 413–423. https://doi.org/10.1037/h0083118

Peterson, D. R. (1976). Need for the doctor of psychology degree in professional psychology. *American Psychologist, 31*(11), 792–798. https://doi.org/10.1037/0003-066X.31.11.792

Pinard, A. (1964). Le modéle scientist-professionnel: Synthesèse ou prothèese? *Canadian Psychology/Psychologie canadienne, 15a*(4), 187–208.

Vipond, D. & Richert, R. A. (1977). Contributions of Canadian psychologists to the war effort, 1939–1945. *Canadian Psychological Review, 18*(2), 169–174.

Wake, F. R. (1958). Report on the Committee on Professional Standards. *Canadian Psychologist, 7*(3), 56–59.

Webster, E. C. (1936). *Vocational guidance in relation to school training and the distribution of mental abilities.* Doctoral dissertation, McGill University. https://escholarship.mcgill.ca/concern/theses/vd66w269z

Webster, E. C. (1939). *Guidance for the high school pupil: A study of Quebec secondary schools.* McGill University.

Webster, E. C. (1941). *Put yourself to the test: A manual of vocational self-guidance.* Harper & Brothers.

Webster, E. C. (1964) *Decision-making in the employment interview.* McGill University Industrial Relations Centre.

Webster, E. C. (Ed.) (1967). *The Couchiching conference on professional psychology.* McGill University Industrial Relations Centre.

Webster, E. C. (1982). *The employment interview: A social judgment process.* SIP Publications.

Webster, E. C. (1988). I/O psychology in Canada: From birth to Couchiching. *Canadian Psychology/Psychologie canadienne, 29*(1), 4–10. https://doi.org/10.1037/h0079757

Weir report on rehabilitation (1943). Repository: Laurier Centre for Military Strategic and Disarmament Studies, Reference Code: CA ON00411 MG-0006-1-1-3.

Wright, M. J. (1974). CPA: The first ten years. *Canadian Psychologist, 15*(2), 112–131. https://doi.org/10.1037/h0081744

Wright, M. J. & Myers, C. R. (Eds.) (1982). *History of academic psychology in Canada.* C. J. Hogrefe, Inc.

Wright, M. (1957). Report of the Committee on Clinical Training. *Canadian Psychologist, 6*(2), 31–34.

INDEX

A

B

C

D

E

Employment Interview 6, 62, 63

F

Ferguson, G. A. 25, 58, 65, 70, 74
Fox, R. E. 12, 16
Fuentes, R. 3

G

Gagnon, A. 34
Graduates 15, 44, 76, 77, 84
Granger, L. 79, 84
Groves, G. P. 21
Guidance and Counselling 73

H

Hawthorne 39
Hebb, D. O. 70, 72, 74
Hitsman, J. M. 52, 64, 66
Howard, James W. 54, 60, 65, 66
Howard, Joseph (Jay) 3, 66
Humphrey, G. 51, 90

I

Industrial/Organizational Psychology 37, 42, 73, 78
Industrial/Organizational Psychology:identity 38
Industrial/Organizational Psychology:role 39
Industrial/Organizational Psychology:training 40
Industrial Psychology 6, 29, 38, 40, 43
Institut de Psychologie 19, 36, 80, 81
Interviewing 49, 56

J

Job Titles 38, 39, 43, 44
J. Walter Thompson 22, 26

K

Kellogg, C. E. 25, 50, 69
Kellogg, P. 42

V

W

Y

Printed in Canada